Card Processing for the Smart Retailer:

Simple Steps to a Better Deal

Paul Martaus

Martaus & Associates

Printed in the United States of America

First Printing, 2018

ISBN: 978-0-692-16978-0

Dedication

For My Wife Dianne

"There ain't no such brand loyalty that a five cents off coupon can't overcome."

Old Retailer Adage

Table of **Contents**

Acknowledgements

A special thanks to Patti, who not only edited this work but provided motivation, advice, insights and a frequent kick in the backside. Thanks also to Tim and Alaine for not only believing in the project but for the continual edits and rereads and to Caroline for the cover artwork and never-ending support.

Foreword

This is a book about the payment processing industry. The business has evolved over the years, changed and morphed on a continual basis. I have been fortunate to have been sitting ringside for many, many years and have witnessed innumerable evolutions, some good and some bad. In all this time, I have held thousands and thousands of one on one interviews with countless players ranging from the movers and shakers directly responsible for shaping the very destiny of the business to mom and pop retailers that manage tiny storefronts and barely get by on their meager sales. It has been exalting at times but humbling most of the time.

The payment processing industry is, on one hand, an incredibly simple business – pick up a transaction over here, deliver it over there and deliver the response back to where it came from. On the other hand, it is one of the most complex and convoluted industries to ever have evolved. In my humble opinion, there is no one, and I mean no one that understands it all. Many know a great deal, but the total picture represents a mystery to all.

Many retailers I have spoken with are absolutely convinced that they have the absolutely best processing deal available in the marketplace. If they believe that, they are one hundred percent correct and I have nothing to provide them. To the others that are always on the hunt for something even slightly better, I have a great deal to offer them. I do not claim to know it all but I do claim to know a lot. This book is dedicated to those smart, hungry retailers that are always open to advice. Enjoy the hunt!

Introduction

IF YOU ACCEPT PAYMENT CARDS, YOU CAN NOT ONLY BENEFIT KNOWLEDGEWISE FROM READING THIS BOOK, BUT YOU MAY GET A BETTER PROCESSING DEAL OUT OF IT AS WELL.

Ever since trade began, commerce has been likened to a kind of warfare. Not in a brutal conflagration way, but more in a strategic, chess match kind of way. When it comes to this type of warfare, the more one understands about their adversaries, the better their chances of success. This book provides the information you, as a smart retailer, need to understand one particular set of adversaries: commercial enterprises that operate, sell, and support payment card acceptance.

When it comes to accepting payment cards, the forces marshalled against you as a merchant are not only imposing, but nearly impossible to beat. They range from the largest banks in the U.S. to small but incredibly talented and motivated sales companies. These organizations have access to nearly unlimited funding, plus the ability to promulgate and change the rules of the game without notification. If as a merchant going up against such an adversary, you can't pull out a win, you should at least aim to survive.

As a merchant accepting payment cards, the forces marshalled against you are imposing and nearly impossible to beat... This book is one that your providers don't want you to read.

I should mention at this point, if you are a retailer who accepts payment cards and are completely happy and satisfied with your current merchant representative, pricing structure, reports, card processor, terminal provider and merchant bank, please put this book down and back away slowly. Consider yourself to be either gifted with tremendous business acumen or are incredibly lucky.

If, however, you are a retailer who accepts payment cards, is always on the hunt for a better deal and you have this niggling feeling that things are not quite right with any aspect of your card processing relationship, please read on – this book contains guidance to help you get that better deal. You may not know it yet, but as a merchant you need all the help you can get because, as noted earlier, accepting payment cards in today's world can be likened to a chess match, one in which you are outgunned.

This is the one book that your service providers do not want you to read. It will expose many of their tricks and provide you enough advice and insight to minimize your costs and your risks. For this is a book about the payment card industry and how it takes advantage of merchants through a complex set of rules and processes it designed to maximize fee income by driving up merchant costs.

If you are a retailer not currently accepting payment cards but actively trying to determine whether or not you should, read this book carefully before signing a contract. Once you accept your first transaction, you are forever subject to a litany of potential problems and issues that no one properly disclosed, and could possibly cost you not only your business but virtually everything you own.

If you are a retailer currently accepting payment cards you probably understand the basics. You settle your point of sale (POS) terminal daily and try to interpret your monthly statements. You probably also recognize the fact that the cost of accepting payment cards keeps going up. And you're asking yourself why. You are not alone.

Merchant card acceptance seems, on its face, a simple business. It is anything but simple, however. And there are few resources readily available or understandable that can help you figure out what you're being charged for or why. The card brands may detail policies and procedures on their websites, but these are presented in thousands of pages of legalese that few merchants have the time or expertise to take in.

I have spent over 30 years consulting with companies involved in card payments. My clients have been many and varied, and have included banks, card companies, processors, terminal manufacturers, and those pesky salespeople who call on merchants with new and better options for card acceptance. Suffice it to say I know a lot about the intricacies of merchant acquiring (clearing and settling card transactions). This book draws on my knowledge, gleaned from participation in hundreds of client strategy sessions, tens of thousands of hours of interviews, and scores of research projects I've performed on behalf of clients. And I still don't know everything.

THE LESSON PLAN

The chapters in this book have been organized to optimize your understanding of the card payment services industry. But a note of caution: the rules and technologies underlying credit and debit cards are not static. MasterCard and Visa, for example, publish new interchange rates every year, and other participants in the process regularly adjust their fees.

Unlike many books of this sort which force you to read the entire work before providing useful insights, I have taken a different approach. All of the necessary steps to follow and decisions you need to get a better deal and to minimize your risk are included in the first chapter. It condenses all of the detailed information provided in the rest of the book so unless you have ample time and interest, you can skip the remainder of the book and go back to work. I assure you however, the devil is in the details as it pertains to this industry, and the more you know the better off you will be in the long run. Those details are in the subsequent chapters I recommend you read them all.

Chapter 1 | The Smart Retailers Checklist gives instruction on how to approach all aspects of your card-acceptance deal. It discusses the merchant contract, what it includes and more importantly what it does not. It presents questions and issues that you must address.

It also provides invaluable information about selecting your POS device, including PCI and EMV security standards, along with other vital information. If these steps are followed, you will have a pretty good handle on where things stand as you search for a better deal from the payment services industry.

Chapter 2 | A Brief History of Payment Cards provides a historical look at the payment services industry and how it evolved into the complex behemoth it is today. Industries like this do not come to life overnight, but grow in fits and starts, adding players and roles as needs arise.

Chapter 3 | Getting to Know Your Adversaries introduces key players that perform the various functions in authorizing and settling card purchases. Each adversary may play one or more roles within the business and these will be identified as clearly as is possible. The payment system infrastructure consists of a patchwork of disparate players, each representing one or more levels of access to that infrastructure. Companies at every level within the infrastructure are allowed to set rules *and fees* for access to those levels and, more often than not, for the lower levels. Many companies buy and sell each other on a regular basis in order to operate on multiple levels at the same time.

Chapter 4 | Payment Cards Explained provides a baseline understanding of a very confusing marketplace. The important points you should take away from this chapter: there are any number of different cards and each entity that issues one or more of these determines all of the rules, regulations and most importantly the fees associated with each.

Chapter 5 | It Costs Me How Much? examines the various components that go into the pricing of merchant card acceptance. This chapter introduces the concepts of Discount, Interchange, dues fees and assessments, and other additions to monthly merchant bills. It provides an overview of the hundreds of levels of Interchange pricing, and strongly advocates the Interchange Plus pricing model above all others. It also identifies the myriad of additional fees that may appear on monthly bills, some of which may be dubious. This is a critically important chapter and requires much concentration and study.

Chapter 6 | What You Need to Know about PCI and EMV addresses the mandatory security initiatives PCI-DSS and EMV and offers a base level of insight and understanding of each program. The payment infrastructure is under constant attack from outside hackers, thieves and even foreign governments. While it is necessary to develop technological responses to protect the viability of the payment services industry, the approach taken, who foots the bills and who is left holding the bag are important considerations for surviving as a card-accepting merchant.

Chapter 7 | Who's that Knocking at My Door? describes the various categories of sales representatives out there trolling the landscape for your merchant card acceptance business. It is important to understand the motivations that drive each specific type of sales rep and, more critically, how they are paid. If you understand what drives the person in front of you, that knowledge may provide some resistance and/or protection to unwary participants.

Chapter 8 | And Along Came the Disruptors describes how innovators with imagination and huge personal or corporate resources have come along to shake things up. Payments innovators have developed entirely new technological approaches to processing transactions and some have even attacked the long held pricing mechanism by offering better, faster and cheaper alternatives. If you are overwhelmed by the traditional approaches, this chapter may offer you another way to go.

Here's a novel idea: instead of paying banks for accessing their card networks, maybe merchants should demand compensation for facilitating bank loans to cardholders

---

Before we move on, I'd like to describe a novel concept I have considered for many years. As a retailer, you provide card issuing banks a tremendous service each time one of YOUR customers uses one of THEIR cards to buy something. If the customer uses a credit card (which is virtually indistinguishable from a debit card) you are in fact facilitating a bank loan to THEIR customer. Shouldn't you be compensated for providing that service? If you sell a lottery ticket or money order, don't you get paid for your troubles? Instead of paying the bank for access to THEIR card networks, you should demand compensation for facilitating loans! This is America and we support free enterprise, don't we?

My primary motivation for writing this book is to provoke thoughts and to provide smart retailers insights as to why merchant costs and risk levels are constantly going up. It delves into the complex nature of the payment services industry, explains why things cost so much, discusses the risks associated with accepting payment cards, and it offers suggestions which, if adopted, could result in cost and/or risk mitigation.

Now let's get down to it. After all, running a business is all about getting the best deal out there!

Chapter 1 | The Smart Retailer's Checklist

This Smart Retailer's Checklist summarizes details presented in subsequent chapters. While this information alone could help lower costs and risks associated with accepting payment cards, the detailed explanations provided in subsequent chapters offer invaluable intelligence on how and why payments companies and their sales partners tilt the playing field to disadvantage merchants like you.

Like many business owners, as a smart retailer you want to spend your money wisely, and money spent accessing the payment infrastructure should be no exception. But too often it is. That's because there are no formal sets of business standards and little oversight of individual participants' pricing practices.

As a smart retailer, you need relevant insights in order to make solid decisions and get on with running your business. Here's a high-level view of gotchas to watch out for.

ANALYZING YOUR DEAL

If you are a retailer who already accepts payment cards, the most logical first question is "What kind of a deal do I currently have – is it bad or good?" The most obvious answer is that there is no way to tell, but you should anticipate that it is more than likely shaded towards the service provider's benefit.

One sure fire way to find out is to ask the industry. Take time out to query one of the countless sales agents who stops by, calls or emails asking if you are satisfied with your current provider. Find out which financial institution and acquirer they represent. Both are written on their business card. If neither is on the card, politely ask them to leave, resting assured they are only there to take your money! Note that many sales agents represent more than one bank and acquirer at the same time, but there will be more on this later.

Once you are comfortable that the agent is legitimate, show them your current deal and disclose that you are not quite sure if you have the best alternative (even if you are). They will gladly come back with an analysis of exactly what is wrong with your current deal. They will also provide you with a proposal to replace your current provider. Take each proposal and run it by at least three other competitors, asking each if they see any weaknesses in each proposal. At the end of the process you will have a pretty good handle on where you stand, the strengths and weakness of your current deal, and the strengths and weaknesses of competitive offers.

This may seem like a lot of work, but I have seen merchants save hundreds of dollars a month by doing just this type of analysis. The best case scenario is you save a ton of money going forward. At the very least, you will be armed with knowledge you can use when it comes time to renew your existing contract.

It is important to emphasize here that disclosing your invaluable business records is not something to be done lightly. I am amazed at how many retailers turn over this data at the mere mention of lower card-acceptance costs. It should only be done as part of a detailed analysis that could yield savings in the long run. Imagine coming home one evening to find your significant other has turned over all of your household financial information including mortgage, credit card, car loan and insurance papers to a stranger that knocked on the door and promised to lower your monthly costs. You get the idea.

YOUR MERCHANT CONTRACT

The contract between a card-accepting business and a merchant services provider is known as the Merchant Processor Agreement (MPA), and it is critical to your business's long term success. The MPA typically ranges from one to nine pages and provides details about you and your organization, details about rates, fees and costs, and most importantly your signature. You will be given a copy of this agreement for future reference. It is critical to have an attorney review the document to ensure you are not signing this agreement with any personal liability in order to protect your precious personal assets.

Be sure to obtain copy of Terms &
Conditions of contract, and review it closely,
with the help of an attorney

Every MPA will undoubtedly reference a terms and conditions portion of the contract, alternately referred to as T&C or Terms of Service. This is a much longer part of the agreement running from 15 to 30+ pages. These are typically very standardized and cover all of the specific details of the agreement, including such matters as the rights and procedures for contract termination and costs and penalty calculations associated with early termination. Because this document is only referenced and not provided to you, you may perceive that your business is not bound by its covenants. This is not the case. Be sure to ask your agent for the T&C document, review it with your attorney and make sure you both understand it thoroughly.

THINGS TO INQUIRE ABOUT AND CONSIDER

If you are considering accepting payment cards for the first time, or even if you're a seasoned pro, the following are critical questions to consider before signing any contract for payment card acceptance services.

1. **What pricing model does the provider offer?** It should be Interchange Plus. If it isn't, insist the provider change to Interchange Plus as soon as it is practical to do so. If you are being charged according to any other pricing model, you are more easily and likely to be cheated. Even Interchange Plus isn't bulletproof, but it is the most transparent and fair model available today. Have an attorney ensure contractually the processor uses the actual published interchange rates for their calculations. Some are known to make up rates.

2. **Does the provider supply reports that break down transaction numbers and amounts by each applicable interchange rate?** This is the only way to truly ascertain how much is being charged. It may be wise to ask for the raw data and have your accountant or bookkeeper write a spreadsheet program that displays it all in an easy to read format. Also, make sure the "plus" portion applied to each Interchange rate appears reasonable, although reasonable can be a flexible term.

3. **What other fees are billed on a monthly basis, and are there any fees not billed monthly?** If so,

what are they, how often are they billed and how are they presented on reports? Be sure to obtain a thorough list of all extraneous charges levied by the various parties involved providing your business with merchant services and how they are reported. Take time to understand what each term means as they can change based on context. If necessary, keep asking questions. If nothing else, you can revel in the fact that you are slowly driving your provider crazy. But seriously, it's important to get a handle on all-in costs, including potentially hidden items that can add up over time.

4. **Does the processor support some effective type of data encryption? If not, when will it be available and fully implemented?** Having a way to prevent data from being read while in transit could save you from losing everything you own because of data breaches. As a merchant, you need a processor that supports some type of solid encryption methodology and your contract should reflect the processor's obligation to do that. Some providers have been known to lie about security capabilities which merchants realize only after being hacked.

5. **Are all installed POS devices PCI compliant? Do they support EMV card acceptance, end-to-end**

encryption, Apple Pay and emerging mobile payment applications? If the answer to any of these questions is no, immediately upgrade to a POS device that meets these requirements, even if it appears incredibly expensive. A POS device meeting these requirements, when coupled with a processor that actually supports end-to-end encryption, could end up saving your business from financial annihilation from fines and other breach-related costs.

6. **What is the timeframe between when POS terminal(s) get settled and when the funds actually post to your business account?** These monies are referred to as "holdbacks," and the timeframe these funds are held can vary dramatically from a couple of days to a month. Processors claim holdbacks provide a level of security against potential chargebacks and possible fraud. Some processors offer same day funding but typically charge significant premiums for the service. It wouldn't hurt to find out the cost and calculate the benefits and costs of gaining access to your funds faster.

7. **How frequently does the processor perform PCI scans, and what does it cost?** Presuming your installed POS device(s) is not a dial-up terminal, PCI scans for vulnerabilities will be performed

automatically by the processor and you will be charged accordingly. Find out how often they are performed, by who, and how much you are charged per scan.

8. **Is it absolutely required to complete and submit a PCI Self-Assessment Questionnaire (SAQ)?** As a card-accepting merchant you must complete the PCI SAQ even if your answers may not make sense. The SAQ offers you, the merchant, absolutely no protection in and of itself, but completing it could save you a ton of money in monthly penalties.

9. **How much are you charged if you do not submit an SAQ?** Processors typically charge a fine of $50 per month until the SAQ is submitted. ISOs have been known to tack on additional fees as well. You may want to determine the fines have been removed upon submission as some conveniently forget to do so when required.

10. **If PCI insurance is provided, who provides it, how much does it cost, and what exactly does it cover?** Many processors and ISOs offer PCI insurance but a number of these insurance plans come with conditions that render them almost useless. For example are those plans that cover a single incident only. Most data breaches include

thousands of payment cards and each card is considered a single incident. Some providers offer self-insured PCI insurance plans providing an out by merely declaring bankruptcy if the incident become too large to cover.

11. **What are the procedures and costs associated with cancelling an existing contract? In particular, what are the charges for early termination?** The specific procedures and costs are typically provided in the Terms & Conditions document referenced in the Merchant Processing Agreement. Be sure to request a copy of the T&C before signing any agreement. Some processors apply incredibly onerous penalties for merchants that terminate contracts early. The upward range could reach tens of thousands of dollars. Currently only one state, Arkansas, actually caps the termination fee ($50) but most providers ignore the statute as it carries no penalties for violation. Check the statutes for states where you operate as this movement may gain traction.

12. **What are the financial consequences of falling short of or grossly exceeding expected monthly transaction volumes?** Many contracts require minimum monthly payments even in months when no card transactions get processed. At the other end of the spectrum, a merchant that

dramatically exceeds expectations will trigger alarms with processors, as huge volume spikes typically are associated with large scale frauds. There have been cases uncovered in the past in which fraudsters were able to run millions of dollars in transactions through individual small merchants in a matter of seconds. It is important to note that as the merchant, you are most likely responsible for these transactions and any associated fees and penalties, which could amount to millions of dollars. Many states have passed laws that also include provisions that could lead to incarceration in such cases.

13. **How and where are funds received from your daily card transactions deposited?** If they are being deposited into your primary business checking account, you may want to open a new account at a different bank to receive those funds. You will also want to move the funds from that secondary account as soon as they are deposited, as merchant banks and Independent Sales Organizations (ISOs) cannot seize funds they cannot access.

14. **How are routine customer service issues handled?** This industry is fairly benign and for the most part everything works as it should. It is important, however, to know who to call after

you're up and running and things do not go as planned. It is also important to know how to escalate things should it become necessary. All processors provide call center support, some using dedicated in-house staff while others outsource the capability. This is important to know, as in-house resources tend to be a bit more responsive to client needs.

POS DEVICES

Irrespective of the age of any existing POS devices you may have installed, if they are not PCI certified, nor EMV compatible, get new devices. EMV—or Europay, MasterCard, Visa—is the international standard for customer authentication established by the card brands. A little known fact about the imposition of EMV, which became mandatory for most U.S. merchants in 2016, is that it shifts all liability to merchants for fraudulent transactions that were authenticated using a card's magnetic stripe instead of its EMV chip. Prior to 2016, card issuers ate at least some of the losses from fraudulent transactions. Today, if you accept a payment card based on its magnetic stripe and the transaction goes south, you eat the loss! Plus associated costs, fines, etc.

Encryption renders the information associated with a payment transaction unreadable from the POS device to the network and back again. If a crook can't read it, they probably won't steal it – or so the theory goes. You may hear about tokenization and similar additional security techniques, and any device that supports encryption technology can be upgraded easily as new methodologies develop.

As noted earlier, compliance with the Payment Card Industry Data Security Standard (PCI, or more formally PCI-DSS) applies to any business that accepts payment cards. Small merchants are required to go on-line yearly to complete Self-Assessment Questionnaires (SAQs) about data security measures. If you have not done so as yet, do so today. The deadlines for compliance have long past and you are being charged a hefty non-compliance fee monthly. You may find some of the questions stupid and confusing but answer them all to the best of your ability, even if it feels like your answer can't possibly be correct. Not doing so will add a steep non-compliance fee to your cost of accepting cards.

Answer the PCI SAQ as best you can. Not completing the SAQ can trigger hefty non-compliance fees

---

A business with a POS terminal that connects to the Internet in any fashion must get that device scanned by a third party company that performs this service. Most processors provide the scan for all Internet supported devices automatically but it is a good idea to ensure that they actually perform the scans. Positive results purportedly ensure that a device has not as yet been hacked. Scans must be repeated on a periodic basis to provide ongoing evidence that devices remain hack free, and rest assured that you will be charged for the service.

If you are hacked, including if one of your employees copies a customer's card information and sells it, you will most likely be forced out of business, charged huge sums of monies, and in some states you could potentially wind up in prison. This is a frightening yet real possible outcome that you must be aware of and prepared for when accepting payment cards.

The PCI standard was developed by the industry to provide some level of protection for cardholders in today's complex on-line environment. Some state governments have codified the standards to ensure retailers comply. Some of these statutes call for fines; others make suffering a data breach while out of compliance a felony punishable by huge additional fines and prison time.

Data security is a moving target and, as a card-accepting merchant, you are most on the hook for hacks

---

The major issue with the PCI-DSS standard is that data security is a moving target and the crooks are smarter, more motivated and better funded than the payment card industry. They find ways around the fixes faster than the fixes can be made part of the standard. From the industry perspective, the easiest solution has been to make you, the merchant, responsible and liable if hacks occur.

You may be able to forestall some problems if your service provider offers PCI insurance. This gets tricky, however, in that insurance policies vary. Many providers self-insure, meaning when it comes time to write a check they may disappear into the woodwork. Others offer "onetime" coverage, meaning that they cover the cost of the first card compromised but not all the cards hacked. If one card number is breached, the fines may only be in the $50,000 to $100,000 range. If many are affected, multi-million dollar fines should be anticipated. Insurance doesn't typically cover these eventualities.

It should be noted that, even if you as a retailer stop accepting payment cards today, you are still liable for data breaches that may have occurred while accepting cards. Some breaches may take years to uncover, but the liability never goes away.

FEDERAL TAX ID NUMBER

Every business has a federal tax ID number. It's important to ensure your service provider has the correct number and the correct spelling of the business name. Many companies have multiple spellings, some may use ampersands, while others spell out "and," and there are similar opportunities for mismatching against federal records. If a card-accepting business's name and federal tax ID are mismatched for any reason, the business is likely to be assessed a fine for not correcting that mistake in a timely manner.

This is also important because service providers are required by the Internal Revenue Service to report the amount of payment activity each client company generates each year. The information is reported on a form 1099. In the near future, the IRS may begin to use that information to impute any revenues a business could be under-reporting, based on a complex mathematical model they are developing. The IRS has said it plans to assess heavy fines for under-reporting as well as levy back tax due amounts. Only retailers that accept cash and checks exclusively are immune to this reporting.

In addition, be on the lookout for any fees a processor may assess for reporting card transaction figures to the IRS. Congress has directed that businesses not bear the costs of collecting and reporting this vital information, but that may not stop some greedy service providers.

IN CONCLUSION

There are undoubtedly innumerable scams and traps being perpetrated by card processors and their sales partners, but the ones described here are the most egregious. The money saving and liability limiting ideas provided are also not complete, but if followed, may at least, lower both your costs and potential liability as a card-accepting merchant.

Even with the intelligence provided here, you may want to secure the services of a consultant or attorney to ensure your merchant contract is a good fit and to help ensure the survival of your business.

Chapter 2 | A Brief History of Payment Cards

The payment card business as we know it today has had a long and colorful past. This chapter provides insights on how the marketplace has evolved to help you understand how to deal with it going forward.

Credit cards have been around since the late 1950's, having first been developed and offered by several major upscale retailers such as Macys, Gimbels and Nordstrom. These retailers had been offering credit to wealthy customers for decades. Following World War II, however, they realized an even larger group of consumers – the emerging Middle Class – was spending a lot of money building comfortable post-war lives. Several retailers started offering pre-approved credit to these consumers, providing metal plates they could present to the store staff to identify themselves and buy goods on credit. The "buy now, pay later" mindset was born as a result.

The impact was huge. At one point, over half of all U.S. households had a Sears credit card. At the peak of its card-issuing dominance, interest earned from the Sears credit card portfolio actually exceeded earnings from goods sold in all of the retailer's stores combined.

Bank credit cards (bankcards) as we now know them evolved because of these major retailer programs. Banks wanted a piece of the action. Bank of America was the first to start issuing cards once it figured out how to underwrite the risk of providing unsecured lines of consumer credit.

BofA also recognized that there were two sides to the newly developed credit card opportunity, consumers and merchants. Based on their risk profiles, the bank offered creditworthy consumers lines of credit that could be used at participating retailers. BofA then went directly to small merchants and offered them access to BofA card-holding consumers.

As the program developed, the bank correctly noticed a competitive imbalance between small merchants and their huge retail counterparts. Small retailers found they could better compete for the business of the emerging Middle Class. For their participation, small merchants would pay a nominal charge ranging from 2% to 4% of the charged ticket to BofA to offset the costs associated with providing them access to pre-approved account holders. Of course, the bank also was eyeballing the huge potential revenue streams flowing from consumers' new outstanding credit balances.

LOCAL PROGRAMS GO NATIONAL

The program was such a success that BofA began offering franchises to the largest banks in major cities around the country. Thus the BankAmericard program was born, which is today known as Visa. Coincidental to this activity, a number of separate groups of banks, consisting mainly of the second largest banks in BankAmericard markets, banded together to found a competing organization and program they named MasterCharge, which evolved into what we now know as MasterCard.

Each of the card brands offered exclusive access to their own card base but also required exclusivity from the retailer. If you were a participating retailer, you either accepted a BankAmericard or a MasterCharge card, but you could not accept both.

As the programs gained traction among small retailers, the brands approached large retailers and offered them access to their burgeoning basis of consumer cardholders. It is interesting to note that because the large retail organizations represented significantly more potential volume than all of the small merchants combined, they were offered lower fees than small retailers. This imbalance remains in place today and continues to be one of the major sources of discontentment among small retailers relative to accepting bankcards.

At the outset, the participating banks quickly realized that while an overwhelming number of consumers used their bankcards locally, a small but growing cadre of mobile clientele were using the cards in cities they visited. So BankAmericard and MasterCharge developed clearing mechanisms that routed the various "foreign" charge slips to accommodate that.

What emerged were elaborate systems that could identify which bank issued a credit card and efficiently route the transaction to that bank so the consumer could be charged for the purchase. These elaborate systems remain in place today, although they have been continually upgraded and updated and no longer use the paper based medium originally put in place.

OPEN VS. CLOSED NETWORKS

As the BankAmericard and MasterCharge card programs grew in popularity, competing independent programs began to evolve, including Diners Club, American Express, Discover, as well as other smaller programs. These programs originally targeted the hospitality industry, including hotels and restaurants, and were popularly known as "Travel and Entertainment" or T&E cards. They were based on what were known as closed loop systems, meaning the cards were issued by the T&E companies. Merchants were solicited to accept the cards and were supported by those companies, and all transactions flowed through authorization and settlement systems owned and managed by the brand-owning companies.

By contrast, the BankAmericard and MasterCharge systems were designed to operate as open loop systems. In these systems, the cards are issued by any number of member banks, merchants are solicited and supported by the member banks, but the authorization and settlement systems are controlled by BankAmericard and MasterCharge. These organizations represented oligarchies in that all the means of production were owned and controlled by a few organizations. The large banking organizations that were the owners wielded the majority of the power and were influenced in small part by smaller franchise owners.

As the card programs gained in popularity, the largest banks developed huge in-house processing systems to support transaction authorization, clearing and settlement. The smaller banks could easily buy their processing resources from the larger banks but many viewed this as a substantial competitive situation and developed independent alternatives in the form of regional processing cooperatives referred to as Bankcard Associations. At the height of their popularity, there were more than 25 such regional processing cooperatives. Over time these cooperatives began to consolidate and became targets for acquisition by independently owned and managed processing companies. None exist today.

TECHNOLOGY, TERMINALIZATION AND FRAUD

Not surprisingly, fraud rapidly became a major issue as card programs grew. The first solution to combat fraud came in the form of booklets, known as "Lost and Stolen Card Bulletins," issued by the card brands. Lost and stolen cards were presented in numerical sequence and retailers had to check each card presented for payment against the list. If the card was not on the list it could be considered valid. A retailer would note on the charge slip the page in the booklet where the card number would have but did not appear.

Over time, looking up cards in multiple booklets proved cumbersome and BankAmericard and MasterCharge moved to combine their bulletins. It became apparent that a new solution was required, and the card brands began an active migration program to on-line point-of-sale terminals.

To spur rapid terminal deployment, the card associations dramatically reduced interchange rates, explaining that on-line transactions were cheaper and faster to process. They also noted that different types of merchants and different types of cards demanded a differential interchange pricing structure. Thus was born the convoluted and completely incomprehensible pricing structure that persists to this day.

In the early days of on-line POS terminals, the devices were quite rudimentary. After the card was swiped, a green light would appear if the authorization was approved and a red light would appear if the authorization was denied. As technologies evolved, an entire sub-industry of custom software providers and value added resellers (VARs) developed, adding yet another layer of complexity to the business.

RISE OF THE ISO

As POS terminal sophistication increased, the financial institutions driving them had to develop even more sophisticated transaction processing systems. Over time, some of the larger institutions determined that developing and supporting complex and expensive transaction processing systems was outside their core competencies, so they outsourced the operations. Yet another sub-industry was born. Like settlement and clearing organizations, transaction processing entities eventually began to consolidate and became popular acquisition targets.

Soon, financial institutions also came to realize that selling and installing POS terminals to millions of small merchants was not one of their core competencies. It became popular to clean house of internal sales forces on a large scale. The former sales executives were offered an opportunity to sell POS terminals and access to the card association infrastructures as commission-based, outside sales agents working on behalf of their former employers. This allowed the institutions to dramatically lower ongoing expenses associated with maintaining in-house sales staff.

The more astute among these former bank employees turned the tables on their former employers by identifying banks that would sell them transaction processing, settlement and other support services on a wholesale basis. They then sold access to these services to the merchant community and pocketed a much larger portion of the Discount fees they charged. Thus the concept of independent sales organizations, or ISOs, was born, adding still another layer of complexity to the business. It is estimated that even in today's small merchant marketplace over 90% of relationships are still managed by ISOs.

RISE OF DEBIT CARDS

As these developments were occurring within the credit card shops of banks and other financial institutions, there were also interesting developments occurring with regard to consumer adoption of personal checking accounts. Until the late 1950s, most American workers were paid in cash, typically on a weekly basis. As the workforce exploded following World War II, bank demand deposit accounts (popularly known as checking accounts) became all the fashion as these allowed customers to draw on the funds deposited by their employers. Employers quickly adopted payroll checks for cash management and security reasons. Retailers began to accept checks from consumers for similar reasons and were even willing to pay service fees to banks to facilitate the process.

Rapid adoption of consumer checking accounts quickly led to a banking system awash in paper. The sorting and clearing of checks became unwieldy. By the early 1960s, banks began to actively develop strategies to deal with this paper nightmare. Automated Teller Machines, or ATMs, were developed to provide consumers with ready access to cash without having to stand in teller lines at banks.

As rapidly as bank-owned ATM networks expanded, consumers found access wanting and began to demand access to machines that were closer to their typical daily commute paths. The solution allowed consumers access to ATMs that were owned and maintained by competing institutions. Banks quickly recognized the revenue potential associated with this solution in the form of shared ATM access fees that they could charge consumers. They formed regional shared ATM networks that developed standards and systems to support interconnectivity between competing financial institutions. Over the years, the regional ATM networks consolidated and today almost all have been acquired by national organizations.

While the regional ATM networks grew, some astute supermarket chains began installing proprietary ATM machines in their stores. They correctly recognized that busy consumers would pay for convenience and began to charge their own access fees while brokering deals with select banks to gain access to the shared ATM networks.

As ATM cards proliferated, retailers further recognized the potential to have consumers use them to pay for their goods at the point of sale. The Food Marketing Institute even went so far as to conduct extensive time and motion studies which concluded that the use of ATM cards in supermarkets yielded faster checkout times, less payment input error, and larger average sales tickets. Some supermarkets were able to convince financial institutions not only to pay for the installation of POS terminals to authorize ATM card purchases but also to pay the retailer a small fee reflecting savings the institution realized from not having to process paper checks. It was a short-lived experiment.

The card companies, by then known as Visa and MasterCard, realized ATM cards were having an impact on credit card usage. Consumers saw that paying for goods and services with money from their checking accounts (using ATM cards) allowed them to avoid credit interest charges. The solution Visa and MasterCard came up was a pricing mechanism that shifted debit transactions from being an expense to a source of revenue for financial institutions.

The solution was to place Visa or MasterCard logos on bank-issued debit cards. In that way, when an ATM debit card was presented to the retailer, the terminal would route the transaction through the Visa and MasterCard authorization infrastructures. Thus the signature-based debit card was born to compete head-to-head with online PIN debit which requires the use of the consumer's Personal Identification Number. Representing a source of revenue as opposed to a cost for banks, signature debit won the competition easily.

Another drawback to PIN debit was that it required separate merchant contracts and a PIN pad, an expensive and possibly complicated piece of additional hardware. In the intervening years, Visa- and MasterCard-branded debit cards grew in popularity to the point where they now generate more dollar volume and transactions than do Visa- and MasterCard-branded credit cards.

Since its inception, the payment card industry has gone through many cyclical changes. Processing on the card issuing side went from almost 100% bank-owned to almost 100% outsourced to the current environment of mixed processing alternatives. Those developments were mirrored on the merchant side. ISOs went from being an exciting alternative to being viewed as incredibly threatening to being accepted as the norm in acquiring merchant relationships for the various players.

Chapter 3 | Getting to Know Your Adversaries

This chapter describes the various adversaries you will have to deal with in order to accept payment cards. There are major adversaries and minor adversaries as well as some auxiliary adversaries.

Here's a short list of major adversaries:

- The Card Associations
- Merchant Banks, including settlement banks and depository banks
- Acquirers
- Merchant Processors
- ISOs
- Card-issuing Banks

Lesser adversaries include:

- Front-end Processors
- Gateway Processors
- Value-Added Resellers (VARs) and Software Providers

- Hardware Providers

Although each of these entities plays a separate role in the payment card industry, many play several roles at a time, and many partner with others to create even more and different roles. This interplay spurs confusion about who is doing what to whom at any given moment.

It should be disturbing to you as a merchant that there are no controls over how your adversaries in this business price their services

---

Perhaps more disturbing to you, as a merchant, is that there are no controls over cost and each adversary is free to charge whatever the market will bear for their services. No wonder the costs associated with accepting payment cards are high and keep going up!

THE CARD ASSOCIATIONS, OR BRAND-OWNING CORPORATIONS

The two most significant companies within the industry are the original card associations, Visa and MasterCard. Each was established as a cooperative bankcard association but both successfully converted to for-profit brand-owning corporations years ago. As bankcard brand owners, each performs two major functions - each determines the rules that dictate all aspects relative to their brand's issuance and acceptance, and each runs extensive networks that facilitate the processing and settlement of transactions made using their branded cards.

In 2017, combined Visa and MasterCards issued in the U.S. (credit, debit and prepaid) generated $4.718 trillion in purchase volume alone according to the February 2018 Nilson Report (issue 1125), a well-respected trade journal. The Visa transaction network processed just under 67 billion transactions worth $3.9 trillion across the U.S. The MasterCard network processed just over 26 billion transactions worth $1.6 trillion in the U.S. As you can see, these two companies generate staggering revenues, making their involvement in the industry significant by definition.

The move from bankcard associations to for-profit brand-owning companies has had significant impact on small merchant costs

From the rulemaking perspective, the brand owners establish systems, card standards, rules and procedures as well as compliance methodologies. They also set interchange pricing and the associated dues, fees and assessments charged to merchant banks—and subsequently passed through to you as a retailer—for supporting the brands. This pass-through arrangement is noteworthy as the brand-owning corporations presume that banks will choose to pass the charges down through their own distribution networks. This arms-length approach provides significant insulation, protection and plausible deniability to the brand-owning corporations. It also helps ensure that all other adversaries within the industry are responsible for compliance with all promulgated procedures and standards, with significant consequences for failure to comply. It also ensures that each succeeding set of adversaries develop methodologies to shift the risk and consequences of non-compliance to those further downstream.

The fact that both companies morphed over time from being cooperative bankcard associations into publically traded corporations has had a significant impact on all other parties associated with the payment services industry, but especially on retailers that accept their branded cards. As cooperative bankcard associations, their actions were dictated and directed by the banks that were equity owners. The early cooperative boards of directors, consisting entirely of member banks, decided on major issues such as pricing and acted more or less as a mitigating body balancing needs and desires of the various interested parties.

As public corporations, the brand owners now find themselves free to "maximize shareholder wealth." Over the past several years they have promulgated significant rules and regulations that have resulted in dramatic shifts of substantial portions of industry revenue streams into their own coffers and away from the other industry participants.

Running parallel to the two brand-owning corporations are non-bankcard providers, and the most notable of these are American Express and Discover. Like the bankcard brand-owning corporations, each of these are independent for-profit businesses. The key difference is that the non-bankcard companies own "closed" issuing, authorization and settlement systems. In other words, each owns all of the means of production associated with their brand, from card issuing on through to the transaction authorization and settlement network infrastructures. Like their larger competitors, each is responsible for brand management, setting rules and regulations for access, as well as establishing systems, card standards, procedures and compliance enforcement methodologies. Unlike the bankcard brands, each deploys an internal sales force to sign up retailers. Recently, however, they have begun to share external sales resources and some network infrastructure with the bankcard brand owners.

MERCHANT (ACQUIRING) BANK

The next important adversaries in the payment card industry are the merchant banks, known interchangeably as acquiring banks. If you accept Visa- and MasterCard-branded payment cards as a retailer, you have been sponsored into these respective networks by a merchant bank. There is no way around that fact. Irrespective of how or who signed you up, you absolutely have a sponsor bank. All you have to do is look on your merchant contract and the name is listed there somewhere, more than likely in the fine print.

Acquiring banks put monies in your merchant accounts. But they can freeze your accounts, too

---

The merchant bank is THE singular entity that is responsible for all aspects of the merchant relationship, regardless of side agreements, codicils, handshakes, semaphore, smoke signals or the like that are designed to shift liability among the adversaries. If something goes awry with your merchant relationship, the acquiring bank is, in the final analysis, totally responsible. In addition, the merchant bank accepts the funds associated with your payment transactions, and tracks those funds through the authorization and settlement infrastructures. The merchant bank can also be where your sales drafts are deposited for settlement.

One important fact to understand about merchant banks is that not only do they have the responsibility to deposit card related monies into your merchant bank accounts, they also retain the right to take funds directly out of those accounts. And they can and will do so without prior notice for a variety of reasons, ranging from periodic fees and assessments to fines associated with rule violations. They also retain the right to freeze all of the funds in a merchant account without prior notice. A surprising number of retailers have no idea this may be the case until it happens, often with dire consequences such as significant overdraft fees and the like.

To add to the confusion, your merchant bank may also be your settlement bank, which receives and consolidates all settlement payment information as well as financial reporting on behalf of you, the merchant; but it doesn't have to be. Your merchant bank may also be your depository bank, which maintains your merchant checking account, or not. The relationship variety is endless and can also change at the drop of a hat for any number of reasons yet to be discussed.

ACQUIRERS

Over the years, the term acquirer has become muddled and confusing. At its core, an acquirer is the organization that takes responsibility for presenting payment transactions to the payment infrastructure and ensuring its proper disposition throughout its lifecycle. In other words, the acquirer grabs the transaction from a POS card terminal when you press the enter button, sends it where it needs to go in the network, and returns the response back to your terminal. And they handle everything in between, either directly or by outsourcing to other players which impose yet more fees.

Although the function of the acquirer has historically been the domain of the merchant bank, a number of other significant adversaries now have the critical mass necessary to successfully don the mantle. Almost all of the adversaries stepping into the role of acquirer are huge ISO organizations that maintain relationships with merchant banks as their sponsors, and many have multiple merchant bank relationships to spread the risk. As pointed out elsewhere, merchant-sponsoring banks are ultimately responsible for all bankcard-related risk, but given the size of these intermediaries, the risk to the sponsoring merchant banks is truly *de minimus*, and the term acquirer is applied liberally.

One feature that distinguishes an acquirer from other adversaries is the access it provides to the Visa and MasterCard authorization infrastructures. This access is provided by unique, proprietary computer systems known as a MasterCard Interface Processor (MIP) and a Visa Access Processor (VAP). The MIP and the VAP computers can only be installed at organizations that fit very strict size and security criteria. To date they have appeared to be bulletproof with respect to hackers and are maintained under strict security protocols.

MERCHANT PROCESSORS

Merchant processors are also referred to as transaction processors. The merchant processor may or may not be affiliated with a merchant-acquiring bank. There are multiple roles for the merchant processor. First, the processor receives transactions from terminal driver and forwards those transactions to the authorization infrastructures for subsequent delivery to the logical authorization databases. Once a response is received either approving the request or denying it, the processor sends the response back to the terminal driving processor. The merchant processor also collects transaction data and can provide some interim reporting to various other industry adversaries.

The merchant processor can also use the transaction data received from terminal driving and acquiring processors to match against financial information associated with the transaction to check the data for anomalies. This provides additional accuracy and auditing checks for the system. At the same time, the processor edits and formats data for the card brand-owning settlement systems and can generate ACH/depository information for merchant banks, and accounting and statement generation for you the merchant.

The merchant processor also receives additional settlement information from association settlement systems, interchange-related data, fulfillment inquiries, and charge-back related information, and can generate periodic billing information for your merchant accounts. All of these are typically fee-based services.

In sum, the transaction processor makes sure cardholders can use their payment cards seamlessly and that you the merchant get paid for their purchases. Behind the scenes, the transaction processor ensures everybody involved gets a full accounting and accurate reporting of transaction information. Simple as that.

INDEPENDENT SALES ORGANIZATIONS

An Independent Sales Organization (ISO) is exactly what it appears to be, an independent company that banks contract with to sell card acceptance and support to merchants. There are several thousand ISOs operating in the market, ranging in size from one-man shops to multibillion dollar corporations. Some estimates suggest these organizations control over 95% of the small merchant market. Collectively, these organizations can be called ISOs, VARs, independent contractors, agents, reps or similar *nom de guerre*. Although the primary focus of an ISO is sales, many provide a wide array of additional support services.

Super ISOs count as clients hundreds of thousands of retailers and are national in scope. They offer a complete array of processing and settlement services. Several super ISOs are actually wholly owned subsidiaries of major banks, and several are partnerships between major transaction processors and major banks. As such, they can also be acquirers with full access to MIP and VAP processing computers.

Next down the food chain are major regional ISOs. These tend to be geographically oriented, and are obviously smaller in scope than Super ISOs. Below them are small local ISOs and what are affectionately known as Mom and Pop ISOs. These smaller ISOs can have merchant portfolios ranging from under a thousand to a dozen merchants. There are no bars to entry into the payment card industry at this level, so many folks are drawn to it because the potential for earnings are unlimited and what rules there are can be easily circumvented.

There is no exact number of sales representatives active across the ISO community but estimates range from ten thousand to over twenty-five thousand. The majority of ISO sales representatives operate on pure commission-based compensation plans although there is a wide range of alternative plans in place across the industry. The relevance to you as a merchant is that the prime motivator for a huge number of sales reps is unbridled greed. A "closer" in this business can easily earn a million dollars a year and many are willing to do or say anything to get your business. I realize this is a hard reality but it remains the truth. Are there honest, hardworking, reputable sales folks out there? No doubt! But there also are plenty that are not.

This behavior, unfortunately, generally flows down from the top of the ISO and is hardwired into the corporate culture. Major companies have regularly encouraged, condoned and rewarded seriously questionable behavior on the part of their sales staffs. They misquote rules and regulations, hide important codicils in their contracts and mislead retailers with no regard to the truth. To top it off, neither of the card-brand owning companies have enforcement capabilities relative to their own rules and procedures. They rely on the banks to do this, and the banks aren't motivated to control their ISOs because violations are typically viewed a victimless crimes.

ISSUING BANKS

The card-issuing bank's role in the acquiring business is multidimensional. As noted earlier, the credit card business has two sides, issuing and accepting. An issuing bank earns tremendous returns lending consumers money via credit cards. To facilitate this, they issue cards to consumers and ensure there are adequate lines of credit available for purchases. Issuing banks provide consumers with their transaction histories in the form of monthly statements. They also manage receivables along with consumer bad debt and fraud exposures.

At the outset, issuing banks wielded tremendous sway over the payment card world. The original bankcard associations were developed and maintained under the auspices of the issuing banks. All board members represented the issuing side. The merchant side of the business represented very minor revenue streams to the parent banks and thus received less management attention.

In today's world, credit cards still account for a tremendous amount of business. In 2017, again as reported by the same Nilson Report (issue 1125), Visa reported having 819 million cards in circulation, MasterCard reported 412 million, American Express had 50 million, and Discover had over 52 million. The industry reported a combined number of accounts as just over 1.1 billion meaning a huge percentage of U.S, households own over a huge numbers of accounts with credit card outstandings of just over $1 trillion.

There is a reason why the issuing side of the bank still holds a lot of power within the card payment industry. Money obviously talks!

FRONT-END PROCESSORS

The majority of small merchants use free standing POS terminals to process card transactions. These terminals must interact with the payment infrastructure in order to facilitate purchases. Front-end processors (FEPs) "drive" these POS terminals and acquire transactions for subsequent authorization processing.

A front-end processor, by definition, has direct connectivity to Visa, MasterCard, maybe Discover and maybe American Express. These systems use the information encoded on the consumer's credit or debit card (either on the magnetic stripe or embedded within an EMV chip) add it to information generated within the POS terminal, translate the accumulated data into a format understandable by the transaction processor's systems and transmit everything to the transaction processor. Upon receipt of a response, the FEP either completes the purchase or provides the denial codes.

The FEP provides and maintains its own transaction processing software and in some cases, provides and supports POS terminal hardware and software. More often than not, FEPs support massive libraries of terminal software releases on behalf of the terminal owners (typically you, the merchant). They also support terminal deployment and ongoing software downloads. If a merchant's POS device requires a reload or an upgrade, the FEP supports that activity.

Additional activities include the collection of daily transaction data, which is subsequently sent to settlement processor(s). Many FEPs provide some level of transaction reporting to assist in daily settlement at the store level, as well as help desk and customer support capabilities. All of these services are typically fee-based activities. Regardless of size or ownership, the FEP is the primary and most immediate physical link between your store and the rest of the payment-card infrastructure.

GATEWAY PROCESSORS

A gateway processor is a transaction processing system that drives terminals and links to one or more front-ends, but does not support direct connectivity to the card brand-owning associations. The distinction is critical in that while there are a fair number of full blown front-end processing systems in the marketplace, gateways are innumerable and everywhere. Most gateways are built utilizing off the shelf "gateway" software that has been thoroughly tested by others and completely PCI certified. These are easily and quickly installed and easily maintained. Many gateway processors support links to multiple acquirer-owned front-end processors and even to other gateways, creating a massive web of interconnectivity.

A primary reason for developing a gateway is to control the process of initiating transaction flows, which by definition converts to control over the relationship with the merchant. Another major reason for developing a gateway is that it offers a significantly more cost effective solution for presenting transactions to front-end providers. Yet another benefit of owning a gateway is that should it become necessary, the gateway can more easily point all traffic to a different front-end, eliminating the need to send new downloads to huge populations of individual POS devices. This flexibility can become priceless should issues develop between a gateway owner and the transaction processor.

Any gateway in the marketplace is viewed as a giant IP transaction concentrator, wherein all dial terminals interact with this gateway, which converts the transactions and presents them to the acquirer's front-end processor as less expensive IP-based transactions.

This cost savings can be passed through to the merchant, but more often than not is pocketed by the gateway owner as reward for their business acumen.

VALUE ADDED RESELLERS AND SOFTWARE PROVIDERS

In the real world, a Value Added Reseller (VAR) buys a product or pieces of products, adds some enhancements and sells it as a different product. In the payment card world, a VAR is a company that provides POS terminal-based technology that supports an industry specific application and adds payment card authorization capabilities to it.

An example would be a beauty salon or a health food store. The owner might buy a computer that takes care of scheduling or inventory, tracks sales and collects information for accounting purposes. The software provider for that computer typically adds the ability to accept payment cards. That software provider is considered a VAR in the payment card world.

The reason VARs are considered as distinct adversaries is because there are a huge number of them supporting hundreds of thousands, perhaps millions, of retailers. Any group that wields that much influence must be considered their own category. A VAR not only develops and maintains the payment application, but in most cases acts as the consultant to you, the retailer, relative to matters pertinent to their software.

The VAR also works closely with ISOs that sell to industry specific groups as a specialty, providing the ISO with a target rich environment. A VAR develops the card payment support and relies on the ISO to market the capabilities for a share of the profits. Large VARs can and do become ISOs themselves. The only danger they present is a potential lack of payment industry security specific knowledge that can keep you, the retailer, out of hot water should the system be hacked.

HARDWARE PROVIDERS

In the context of this book, the discussion of hardware providers is limited to POS terminal manufacturers. Every merchant has a POS device on their countertop or embedded within their cash register system somehow. It is the responsibility of the POS terminal manufacturer to ensure the device you purchase meets the PCI-DSS security standards and is capable of interacting with an EMV chip card. They do so with a combination of hardware and software features designed to meet these standards.

*Upgrading the hardware in installed devices
is difficult, if not impossible*

Once installed, it is difficult, if not impossible, to upgrade the hardware in the field. Software updates are a different matter. Presuming the device is connected to the Internet, the manufacturer merely downloads a new upgraded software package to address new standards and requirements. What makes it more difficult is when you, as a merchant, contract with a third party to implement special added code to your POS device to meet some specific need of your own design or requirement. A software upgrade from your POS manufacturer may override your special code or, in some cases, render the POS device inoperable until things get straightened out.

When you add in the complexities surrounding having sold hundreds of thousands of terminals running thousands of different releases of software and untold number of special add-on patches, the issue becomes much more crystalized. It may behoove you to keep in regular contact with your hardware manufacturer just to keep your business running smoothly.

Several key POS manufacturers have also developed FEP systems in an attempt to develop recurring revenue streams. These are solid offerings but keep in mind that using one tends to lock in your options going forward.

Chapter 4 | Payment Cards Explained

The U.S. marketplace is home to a dazzling and totally confusing array of payment cards. There are:

- Branded (logoed) credit cards
- Secured credit cards
- Business credit cards
- Travel & Entertainment cards
- Bank-Issued debit cards
- Decoupled debit cards
- Private-label credit cards
- Prepaid debit cards

These cards are issued by a variety of companies, each of which promulgates rules and procedures for accepting their specific set of offerings by merchants. This is important to know in order to grasp the magnitude of issues faced when determining which cards to accept.

BRANDED PAYMENT CARDS

Branded credit cards are issued under the auspices of the credit side of any given bank. Federal rules for bank-issued credit cards fall under Regulation Z (which implements the Truth-in-Lending Act). Logoed debit cards are issued by the checking account side of banks, and are tied to, consumer checking accounts. These cards fall under Regulation E (which implements the federal Electronic Funds Transfer Act). The distinctions are important only when something goes wrong, as you'll soon understand.

Logoed credit cards display either the Visa or MasterCard brand. At one time, they were the primary type of card used by U.S. households. According to creditcards.com, as of 2014, there were 304 million Visa credit cards and 285 million MasterCard credit cards in circulation in the U.S. But these are not all alike. Each brand supports a variety of different credit cards (e.g., plain vanilla, rewards, business…), and each of these impose different acceptance rules and interchange rates.

Visa- and MasterCard-branded cards are typically issued by banks, credit unions and similar companies under license from Visa and MasterCard. As noted previously, Visa and MasterCard promulgate all of the rules, regulations, policies and procedures associated with the issuing and acceptance of cards bearing their logos, as well determine and levy fines for violations of those rules, regulations, policies and procedures. The monitoring and enforcement of those rules is the responsibility of those institutions that issue the cards. Visa and MasterCard fines actually get levied against the issuing or acquiring banks directly, which in turn pass the fines downstream to the offending party. This convoluted system holds the brand-owning companies fairly harmless from blowback since they appear to be operating at arms-length.

FROM PLAN VANILLA TO REWARDS

Plain vanilla credit cards are attached to lines of credit. Each cardholder is provided a line of credit reflecting the risk the issuer is willing to accept, as determined by credit scoring companies. These cards are typically high interest, low credit line cards offered to young, first time borrowers or to lower income households that meet the minimum underwriting guidelines.

As a cardholder's creditworthiness increases, an issuer will tend to spice up their offerings by lowering interest rates slightly, increasing credit lines slightly and coloring the cards to make them appear more exclusive. Thus there are gold cards, platinum cards, ruby cards, gentian violet cards, etc. The more precious the underlying mineral or more obscure the color, the more prestigious the offering. Issuers only make these prestigious cards available to select customers, maintaining their air of exclusivity. From your perspective, as a merchant, these card offerings typically involve the same pricing scenarios.

Rewards cards cost more to process and business rewards cards represent the most expensive alternative, primarily due to the additional information that must be passed back and forth between the merchant and processor.

Rewards cards award points, on a periodic basis and in direct proportion to the dollar amount the cardholder spends. There are several subcategories of rewards cards that offer points towards travel, gasoline, merchandise and/or services, cash rebates or a plethora of combinations limited only by the marketing genius of the card-issuing organizations. Of course, someone has to pay for the underlying rewards programs, and the issuers have decided that retailers are easiest to glean extra revenues from on an ongoing basis. Thus rewards cards cost more to process, although from a technological standpoint they are identical to other consumer credit cards.

SECURED CREDIT CARDS

There is a body of consumers that do not have sufficient credit histories or high enough credit scores to qualify for any type of credit card. Behavioral studies have indicated that many of these consumers wish to appear to be "typical" consumers by participating in the POS purchase experience. The card brands have designed the secured credit card to fulfill this need by having the consumer deposit funds into a dedicated account at a member bank that will then issue a branded card with a purchase limit lower than the amount on deposit. Satisfactory purchase histories can in some cases lead to positive credit scores leading in turn to qualifying for an unsecured credit card.

BUSINESS CREDIT CARDS

Business credit cards are issued to businesses rather than individuals and, like consumer cards, come in several subcategories and flavors, with rewards cards being the preferred offering. Many businesses use these cards to pay for a wide range of goods and services in order to maximize the rewards points which they use to provide bonuses to executives and employees.

It is incredibly important to learn as much you can about business cards because the cost of accepting a business card is substantially higher and more complex than accepting typical consumer cards. The justification for higher costs is the fact that, in theory, more information about the purchase has to be provided to the card issuer and obviously more information requirements equate to higher costs. The fact that the terminal program collects the overwhelming majority of the required information and the fact that the interceding computer programs fill in the missing blocks does not appear to mitigate the cost factors. This is just something to keep in mind.

GENERAL PURPOSE CREDIT CARDS

A category similar to branded credit cards is what has been traditionally called T&E, or travel and entertainment, cards and were originally tailored to support those activities, namely travel and entertainment. In the modern vernacular, they are also referred to as general purpose credit or charge cards. These cards in today's world are more than likely issued by either American Express or Discover. They differ from traditional credit cards in that they are referred to as closed loop cards. This means that, for the most part, Discover or American Express controls distribution and acceptance processing of their own cards. Recent changes in acceptance methodology and practice provides access to the open loop infrastructures to these cards but for the most part they can still be considered closed loop cards.

BANK-ISSUED DEBIT CARDS

Debit cards provide cardholders with access to funds in their checking accounts at regulated financial institutions. Many financial institutions issue debit cards coincidental to checking account opening. Debit cards have become increasingly popular with consumers and businesses alike. In recent years, total POS payments using debit cards with Visa and MasterCard logos have in fact outnumbered total Visa and MasterCard credit card payments.

Like credit cards, bank-issued debit cards can be tied to rewards programs. Today, the single most expensive card for you as a merchant to accept is a business rewards debit card.

As a retailer, you will only ever see debit cards that carry a Visa or MasterCard logo. Banks occasionally issue debit cards to customers without either logo, but those are for use only at ATMs. When a customer presents a logoed debit card for a purchase, you as a merchant have two processing alternatives available: a PIN-based debit transaction or a signature-based credit transaction. The consumer, however, decides which method is used by pushing the appropriate button on the POS terminal.

When the PIN-based alternative is selected, the customer types their PIN directly into the terminal or via a separate PIN pad. The transaction then flows through the debit networks to a file that represents the consumer's checking account balance for authorization.

When the credit alternative is selected, the transaction flows through the credit card networks to a different file that also represents that consumer's checking account balance. Neither the debit network file nor the credit network file actually represents the real balance in the consumer's account, but rather a near approximation of the balance.

For marketing purposes, banks generally represent debit transactions as being "real-time," although the funds may not come out of the cardholder's account for several days. The same holds true for credit transactions. In the case of debit, the cardholder may no longer have the funds available when the transaction is settled, but the bank stands ready to "lend" them the required monies for a fee.

DECOUPLED DEBIT CARDS

Decoupled debit cards are a unique and unusual payment alternative and are not issued by a bank. Several major programs have been implemented by a few larger retailers, such as Target, and by American Express with their OptBlue program. A decoupled debit card allows consumers to access funds in their checking accounts using a card that has been issued by an organization other than their bank. The actual payment takes the form of a draft withdrawal against the consumer's checking account rather than a demand for payment, but uses the traditional credit and debit networks for processing.

PREPAID DEBIT CARDS

Prepaid debit cards were created as electronic alternatives to traditional paper gift certificates which had become susceptible to counterfeiting. They have become very popular with consumers, and are issued by banks, nonbank financial companies and retailers. The primary drawback of merchant-owned and operated prepaid card programs is they often require separate on-line systems to support the use of a different POS terminal for authorization than the one used for credit and debit cards.

An extremely popular and profitable proprietary prepaid scheme is the Starbuck's program. Starbucks is on record as stating their prepaid program is second only to Frappuccinos in profitability.

The card brand companies eventually developed a more universal solution, placing their already popular Visa and MasterCard logos on prepaid cards. Consumers purchase and load money onto the cards; each is carried as a reducible value on the respective network. Branded prepaid cards can be used at any retailer that accepts Visa- and MasterCard-logoed credit and debit cards. Many variations have evolved that allow retailers to put their logos on prepaid debit cards in order to drive business into their locations. These co-branded cards are very popular and their use is becoming widespread.

Prepaid cards with the Visa and MasterCard logos also have been widely adopted by unbanked Americans as an alternative high-cost checking accounts.

PRIVATE-LABEL CREDIT CARDS

Private label credit cards are those that are issued by a major retailer directly to their customers for use only within their store locations. As noted in the chapter on the history of the industry, the most famous private label program is the Sears card. At its zenith every other household in America had a Sears card in their possession, and Sears made more money annually from credit card interest than it made on all of the sales of goods across its entire chain of stores.

The major drawback to private-label credit card programs is that they require proprietary authorization, settlement and billing systems, which are expensive. In today's hacking environment, data and network security can also become a nightmare scenario. Third party processors have developed over the years to manage these requirements but they are an expensive alternative.

Today, most of the private label card programs have been supplanted by so-called co-branded cards. Co-branded cards prominently display the name of the retailer on the face of the card along with a Visa or MasterCard logo. These cards are more popular with consumers because they can be used everywhere the card brands are accepted. Retailers prefer them because they perceive that cardholders will be subliminally reminded of the retailer every time the card is pulled out of the wallet.

Chapter 5 | It's Costing Me How Much?

Very few retailers have a clear understanding of how much accepting payment cards actually costs them on a monthly basis. Even your Merchant Processor Agreement (MPA) offers very few clues, as cost is a moving target and service providers have absolutely no incentive to make it easy to understand. The industry's operating philosophy appears to be "the less you know, the more you can be charged!"

There are three major considerations when determining the true cost of card acceptance:

- Individual Cost Components
- Pricing Model
- Reporting Options

But don't be fooled: it's not as simple as it may seem. Although cost components are typically represented as fixed, they can and are often misquoted up front or altered without notice. There are numerous pricing models and almost all of them can be easily manipulated. Plus reporting can easily obscure not only costs but many types of exceptions that drive up costs, and there are few, if any, associated audit trails.

COST COMPONENTS

It is important to remember that you, as a merchant, are not really charged for Interchange, dues, fees and assessments by the card-brand owning corporations. It is the member banks that get charged these amounts. They, in turn, pass the charges through to their agents who, in turn, pass them on to you, the merchant. As the fees are passed along, each player has an opportunity to do so at par or, more than likely, add a small amount to cover their costs and troubles.

As a merchant you pay a Discount;
Interchange is just one component of the
Discount fee

While the term Interchange has become synonymous with how much you, as a merchant, pay for card processing, in actuality, you pay a "Discount" for said access. And the Discount fee calculates out to be a significantly higher amount than Interchange. It has also become conventional wisdom to identify Interchange as the "wholesale" cost of processing and Discount as the "retail" cost of processing, but there is a lot more to it.

DISCOUNT

Discount includes not only Interchange but also a transaction fee; brand-mandated dues, fees and assessments; plus a healthy profit margin. More often than not, you, the merchant, are also charged a bevy of additional fees on a monthly and/or quarterly basis, concocted and assessed by various parties involved in providing you with payment processing services. Keep in mind that there are a huge number of players involved in providing merchants like you with access to card payment systems, and each of them has to exact a price for their efforts in order to remain in business.

Keep in mind that there are a huge number of players helping merchants access the card networks, and each has to make money to stay in business

Often service providers have little understanding themselves of the entire industry pricing mechanism. Instead they receive price lists for the services they sell and/or provide on behalf of upstream providers. Every additional provider adds on what they consider a fair markup for their part in the process.

INTERCHANGE

Interchange is one of the biggest single cost elements of the discount fee that is applied to each transaction. Simply put, Interchange is the portion of the Discount that is sent directly to the card-issuing bank to reimburse that bank for issuing a card that consumers use to access their credit or checking accounts to pay for goods and services at your checkout. Simple as that.

In the early days, Interchange was fairly easy to calculate and rationalize as it only involved credit card accounts. When a card-issuing bank sends you, the merchant, money on behalf of the cardholder to reimburse you for cardholder purchases there is a real cost associated with that process. The cardholder has promised to pay the issuing bank, either in full when they receive their bill, or over time. When the industry was in its infancy, payment processing was so cumbersome it often took up to 45 days for a charge to be posted and presented in a statement issued to the cardholder. The cardholder then had a *grace period* during which they could remit payment in full or to start accruing interest on an extension of credit.

The amount of time from when the issuing bank sent you, the merchant, money and when they either received payment in full or began charging interest could be calculated, and the issuing bank would be compensated for the cost of having that money outstanding. This was not magic, just math. The issuing bank was even paid a bit more to assume the risk that their cardholder would not repay the money lent, and that amount could also be calculated based on historical norms.

And then along came on-line POS terminals. The entire payment processing mechanism sped up so dramatically that issuing banks could provide cardholders with statements almost overnight, although historical patterns still supported 30-day billing cycles. Faster processing also supported instantaneous charging of interest, which was waived if a cardholder paid balances in full each month.

On-line authorizations also dramatically reduced the element of risk. Traditional Interchange calculations went out the window, as did the rationale for charging Interchange. But norms are hard to challenge, so the industry just put down their collective heads and charged ahead.

Unable to rationalize Interchange pricing through mathematics, the card brands justified Interchange as a means of recouping their investments in technologies, processes and people that support cheaper transaction processing. They even lowered many Interchange rates to encourage merchants to adopt the use of on-line POS terminals. This practice became known as "incentive" Interchange pricing. Incentive pricing is still used today when the brands decide to spur card acceptance in particular vertical markets, like health care providers. Today, Interchange pricing no longer has a basis in reality, nor does it reflect actual costs.

Today, Interchange has no basis in reality,
nor does it reflect actual costs

In theory, Interchange should be able to be determined by consulting documents available for download from the different card brand owning corporations.

In each document, you will find sets of matrices consisting of three components – card type, along with a combination of transaction type and merchant type. Just cross reference each card type with transaction type and merchant type and see what each will cost. Nothing to it, any retailer could easily understand that. If you delve deeper however, things are not that straightforward. And there's plenty to delve into.

The Visa document is 18-pages long and contains 9 sets of matrices. MasterCard's version is 10-pages long and contains 11-sets of matrices. The Visa matrices cover 18 different card types and MasterCard's cover over a dozen. These types vary from debit to credit to prepaid to corporate and, finally, to commercial cards. They also differentiate between standard, preferred and rewards cards.

As a merchant, you should be aware that there are over 30 different card types, each of which may or may not have different associated Interchange rates. Many cards bear a striking resemblance to each other, so telling them apart at the point of sale is problematic. Not that it matters as you probably won't want to differentiate anyway, as every card represents a sale, irrespective of the cost. And remember, card type is only one factor in overall costs.

The other two factors contributing to Interchange rates are intertwined as a combination of transaction type and merchant type. Transaction type refers to how the transaction is processed, e.g. fully-qualified swiped or key entered. Merchant type is almost self-explanatory and is mostly based on the Merchant Classification Code (MCC) which is derived from the Standard Industry Classification (SIC) code system used by the federal government. "Mostly-based" is a euphemism meaning that the card brands have also applied additional unexplained conditions and/or requirements for certain merchant types to the overall pricing mix.

Keep in mind whatever fantastically attractive rate you originally were quoted is the one least likely to show up on your monthly account statements

---

Needless to say, there are innumerable combinations that yield a wide variety of Interchange rates that can be imposed depending on many different conditions. In actuality, you may never see more than a dozen or so on your billing statements because the majority of rates do not apply to small merchants. Suffice it to say that the higher ranges of rates are applied to small merchants because you, as a group, wield the least amount of market influence. What's important to keep in mind is that whatever the fantastically attractive rate that was quoted before you signed up for a merchant account is the one least likely to actually show up on your monthly merchant account statements.

THE LOW DOWN ON DOWNGRADES

Another important set of factors impacting overall costs are transaction downgrades. You, as a merchant, are consistently promised very attractive Discount rates for "fully qualified" transactions. These are typically transactions that are electronically submitted, authorized and settled. The customer must be present and the transaction must be settled in a timely manner. But transactions can and do fail to meet these narrowly constructed criteria, resulting in downgrades which trigger higher Interchange and Discount rates.

These would include more expensive card types, such as rewards cards or those that potentially carry a higher risk of fraud or non-payment, which often get downgraded to "mid-qualified." Business or international cards which potentially carry even higher risks than rewards cards and those that are manually entered get downgraded to "non-qualified," and are subject to the highest Interchange and Discount rates.

While this may not seem important on the surface, most processors fail to disclose that the majority of transactions (in some cases as many as 80%) are either downgraded to mid or non-qualified. Presuming you are a typical small merchant, downgrades can cost you upwards of an additional $500 to $1,000 per month with little explanation. Not only are downgrades costly, but no audit trails or rational explanations are required for downgrades.

The biggest issue with downgrades (besides the horrendous costs) is the lack of audit trail or rational explanation as to what triggered a downgrade

---

The downgrade phenomenon brings to light yet another strange practice within the card processing universe. The card-issuing bank provides the card to the consumer and the merchant processors provide the authorization infrastructure. Yet, if any piece of the process fails to work, it's you, the merchant, who pays in terms of higher fees and lost productivity. In other words, when their cards or equipment fails, it's you, the merchant, who foots the bill.

DUES, FEES AND ASSESSMENTS

Dues, fees and assessments are set by the card brands and passed along to merchants by acquirers and their ISOs. They vary by brand and are charged either as a percentage of the transaction amount or on a per item basis. These fees ostensibly cover costs associated with providing a dedicated, secure network, but many see them as a source of free money to the card brand owning corporations.

The fees listed below are by brand. They change periodically, usually upwards. It is important to note that although the card brands levy these fees across the board, processors and ISOs typically mark up assessed amounts to bolster their own earnings.

Although the card brands levy fees across the board, processors and ISOs typically add markups

---

Visa Fees

Acquirer Processing Fee (APF) – Credit $0.0195 – Debit $.0155

Credit and Debit Assessment Fee - .13% (applied to gross credit and debit dollar volume)

Credit Voucher Fee – Credit $0.0195 - Debit $0.0155 (transaction fee for refund transactions)

Fixed Acquirer Network Fee (FANF) – Variable, based on complicated formula that factors in processing method, number of locations and transaction volume. FANF fees for small merchants typically range from $2.00 to $9.80 per location per month

International Service Assessment Fee - .80% (applies to U.S. transactions paid for with a card issued outside of the U.S. and settled in U.S. dollars); 1.20% on transactions settled in currencies other than U.S. dollars

International Acquirer Fee - .45% (applies under the same circumstances as the International Service Assessment Fee noted above)

Kilobyte (KB) Access Fee - $0.0047 charged on each authorization transaction submitted to Visa network for settlement

Misuse of Authorization Fee - $0.09 assessed on Visa authorizations not followed by matching clearing transaction

Settlement Network Access Fee - $0.0025 assessed on all U.S.-based settlement transactions

System File Transmission Fee - $0.0018 applied to all Visa transactions

Transaction Integrity Fee (TIF) -$0.10 charged on all Visa debit and prepaid card transactions that do not meet CPS requirements

Zero Dollar Verification Fee - $0.025 charged when a cardholder's information is verified without actually authorizing a purchase amount

Zero Floor Limit Fee - had $0.20 applied to settlement transactions submitted without a proper authorization

MasterCard Fees

Account Status Inquiry Fee - $0.025 assessed when a merchant requests validation for address verification service (AVS), card validation code (CVC2), or both

Acquirer Brand Volume Fee - .14% applied when transaction amount exceeds $1,000 (signature debit card transactions excluded)

Acquirer License Fee (ALF) - .0045% assessed on gross MasterCard processing volume

Acquirer Program Support Fee - .85% applies under the same circumstances as the Cross-Border Assessment Fee for U.S. transactions (see below)

Address Verification Fee - $0.0075 for Card-Not-Present, $0.005 for Card-Present transactions charged each time merchant accesses AVS when processing a transaction

Card Validation Code 2 (CVC2) Transaction Fee - $0.0025 applied to all U.S. card transactions with the CVC2 (three digit code on the back of card) included in the transaction for authorization

Credit and Debit Assessment Fee - .12% applied to gross credit and debit transaction volume

Cross Border Assessment Fee (Domestic) - .60% assessed when U.S. transaction is initiated with card issued outside U.S. and settled in U.S. Dollars.

Cross-Border Assessment Fee (Foreign) - 1.00% assessed U.S. merchants settling international transactions in currencies other than U.S. Dollars

Digital Enablement Fee - .01% assessed on total of card-not-present sales

Kilobyte (KB) Access Fee - $0.0044 charged on each authorization transaction submitted to MasterCard network for settlement

Merchant Location Fee - $15 per location, billed annually

Network Access and Brand Usage Fee (NABU) - $0.0195 applied to U.S.-based authorization and refund transactions

Processing Integrity Fee - $0.055 applied to Card-Present, Card-Not-Present, No reversal transactions with some merchant classified as exempt as follows:

- Card-Present: transactions that are not settled, cleared, or reversed within 24 hours of the original authorization transaction/request;

- Card-Not-Present: transactions that are not settled, cleared, or reversed within 72 hours of the original authorization transaction/request;
- No Reversal: transactions that cannot be matched to corresponding settlement records for over 120 days.
- Exempt merchants: Travel and entertainment merchants classified as MCC 3351-3441, 3501-3999, 4411, 7011 and 7512 are exempt from the Processing Integrity Fee

Yearly Registration Fee - $500.00 assessed solely on e-cigarette/vaping businesses

Discover Card Fees

Discover Assessment- .13% applied to gross value of Discover card transactions

Data Usage Fee - $0.0195 assessed all U.S.-based authorization transactions

Network Authorization Fee - $0.0025 for each Discover network authorization

International Processing Fee - .55% assessed for transactions initiated using cards issued outside of the U.S.

International Service Fee – .80% assessed for U.S. transactions initiated using cards issued outside of the U.S.

American Express Card Fees

American Express Assessment/Sponsorship Fee - .15% applied to gross value of American Express card transactions

Card-Not-Present (CNP) Surcharge - .30% applied to gross value of CNP transactions (e.g.: keyed and e-commerce transactions) in addition to assessment/sponsorship fee

International Assessment - .40% applied to gross sales volume of from cards issued outside the U.S.

PRICING MODELS

There are a variety of pricing methods employed in the merchant acquiring business and all can be easily manipulated to ensure that you, the merchant, are taken advantage of on an ongoing basis. The most common pricing models are:

- Interchange Pass-Through
- Interchange Plus
- Interchange Plus-Plus
- Tiered

- Blended
- Enhanced Rate Recovery, also known as Enhanced Bill-Back

Interchange Pass-Through is a fixed-rate model that adds a flat per-item charge and a flat basis-point surcharge to each transaction on top of Interchange and associated dues, fees and assessments. It represents the most honest and straightforward pricing method in that it is completely transparent. What you see is what you pay. This pricing model is nearly impossible to find in the marketplace. Although processors support straight pass-through, few offer it as a pricing option.

Interchange Plus is similar to straight pass-through, except it includes a premium to protect the processor against more risky transactions. Interchange Plus pricing is becoming more common in the market, although many processors would rather merchants not choose any of the Interchange dependent pricing options.

Interchange Plus-Plus is the latest variation on the Interchange Plus theme and allows less scrupulous providers to not only add basis points and pennies to Interchange, but also to dues, fees and assessments as well. Unfortunately, given the nature and obscurity of this latter portion of the fee structure, processors can load fees with inordinately large add-ons as merchants have no baseline against which to check them. As a result, many merchants see huge increases in the amounts charged without recourse.

Tiered pricing was once the most commonly used pricing alternative. Tiered pricing uses multiple "buckets" into which various transactions are dumped as they are processed. As explained previously, an average of fewer than 40% of card transactions meet the criteria to be assessed the nominal rate. The other 60% are "downgraded" according to risk and other factors pretty much at the discretion of processors. The minimum number of "buckets" is three, representing fully qualified transaction, mid-qualified (mid-quals), and non-qualified transactions. However, there can be innumerable buckets each with an assigned but undisclosed rate based on a number of obscure and unfathomable criteria. Processors count on these downgraded transactions to drive profitability, although they rarely disclose the higher rates, or how or why a particular transaction is downgraded.

Blended pricing was once popular but has fallen out of favor. It was sold as the easiest rate to understand because it theoretically averaged the mix and number of transaction types and produced one straight forward discount rate. Every transaction cost the same. The most obvious flaw was in the original calculation of the mix and number of transaction. Most processors applied higher percentages of more expensive transaction types, tilting the profitability in their favor. But most didn't properly account for changing market conditions and frequent increases in Interchange rates, resulting in unprofitable returns. Hence its downfall.

Enhanced Rate Recovery (or Enhanced Bill-Back) is a pricing method that purports to be one low Interchange rate for all transactions processed in a given month. This allows the provider to tout a very low processing cost. The enhancement part comes into play at the end of each month, and that's when the cost rises. The processor goes back through the month's transactions to determine which were processed as fully qualified and which were downgraded. Downgraded transactions are then accumulated and the appropriate higher rates applied to each, minus the fully qualified rate assessed originally. These transactions are then listed as processed and identified as billed-back transactions. The net amount of the differential is calculated and deducted from the merchant's account. The problem with this approach is obvious: you, the merchant, are provided only the net amount and no detailed information regarding how the amount was calculated. The lack of any audit trail makes this the most egregious pricing method in the market today!

Remember: Although Interchange is based on numbers that have been written down somewhere, Discount resides in the imagination and creativity of the processor.

LEGITIMATE REQUIREMENTS AND FEES VS. POSSIBLE SCAMS

Merchant acquiring is complex. There are countless variables involved in terms of pricing models, processing arrangements, service providers and other costs of doing business. This creates opportunities for unscrupulous players to invent scams to relieve merchants of their hard-earned dollars. I am not a lawyer, and I do not represent what follows as legal advice. I do, however, offer examples of decisions I would make in various situations. They may or may not apply to your particular situation.

With that in mind, these are some programs and fees that can be legitimate but in most instances should be avoided if possible.

Application Fees. Any provider that requires an application fee should be avoided. Access to the payment card infrastructure is expensive enough on an ongoing basis.

Early Termination Fees. This one is tricky. If you choose to leave your existing provider, that provider is required to maintain your business's MID on an inactive file for 6 months, which costs $60. Many providers charge a lot more than $60, however, when a merchant terminates an agreement early. The most egregious calculation includes an average monthly revenue figure anticipated through the remaining life of the contract, which can result in termination fees totaling tens of thousands of dollars. Many providers charge between $350 and $1,000. Others are more reasonable. Some providers even offer to buy out your contract and pay the termination fees on your behalf in exchange for your business.

Terminal Lease Options. Leasing a POS terminal makes little financial sense. A three year terminal lease for $40 per month will end up costing you $1440. The same terminal likely can be purchased online for as little as $300.

Free Terminal Programs. There is no such thing as a free terminal. You will end up paying for it through hidden fees over the life of the merchant contract.

Access to Merchant Account. This should be a red flag. Some providers include provisions in merchant contracts allowing them to access merchant bank accounts. Be sure to have an attorney scrutinize your merchant acquiring agreement and remove any contractual right for the provider to access your bank account.

Reserves/Holdbacks. Providers require merchants to leave certain amounts of money on deposit in one of their accounts to cover risks. Although there is a certain amount of logic to this practice, the reserve amount is still *your* money. Negotiate vigorously to keep this amount as small as possible.

Delayed Funding/Increased Settlement Times.
Providers will often stretch out the amount of time they hold a merchant's money in order to increase their profitability and lower risks. Often this can amount to days and even weeks. The practice of "same day funding" is beginning to be adopted, slowly, by the industry, for a premium charge, of course.

Delayed Adjustments. Similar to delayed funding, providers often take extra time managing adjustments and take more time funding those adjustments once they arrive. The longer they can delay, the higher their profitability. Keep an eye out for these, as there are rules against such practices, and the costs to you as a merchant will add up over time.

Supplies. Merchants are sometimes charged for supplies necessary to advertise and manage card acceptance. This is crazy. You shouldn't pay to advertise others' products. If the provider and the brands want folks to know you accept their cards, they should provide these supplies free of charge.

Merchant Club. A variation on the supply scam, some providers charge a monthly fee to provide supplies, "elite" customer service, etc. These all should be provided free!

PCI Certification Fees. As discussed in the chapter "What You Need to Know about PCI and EMV," providers will often charge a monthly fee of $5 to $10 to cover their cost of having to support PCI. This is a mandated program and once you, the merchant, complete the SAQ there should be no monthly fees. If you fail to complete the SAQ, these monthly fees can skyrocket to $50 or higher.

PCI Insurance. In theory, PCI insurance can be a good thing, provided the program is managed by a legitimate third party insurer. Exceptions include provider self-insured and single occurrence programs. PCI violations rarely involve one card and card-issuing banks have been known to illegally "pile-on" card numbers not involved in an occurrence to clean up bad accounts that have been lying around.

Promises of access to cash advances in exchange for application. Some providers have been known to offer access to extra capital funding that is dependent upon completion of a merchant account application. If you as a merchant need capital that badly, the provider already knows and is trying to push you off the cliff a little faster.

Personal Endorsement. In all likelihood you have a corporation to protect your personal assets should your business be forced to close its doors. Direct your attorney to remove any language from your merchant contract that requires a pledge of personal assets to secure the relationship.

Monthly Fees. Providers will often bill merchants for various and sundry monthly fees that are unidentifiable, or they inflate legitimate monthly fees. Keep an eye out for things that appear out of whack.

Telecommunication Fees. Providers will often add a hefty monthly fee for support of telecommunication services, although no individual costs are incurred. Providers receive telecom support free of charge as part of the package of services provided by upstream partners.

Reporting Fees. Providers will often assess a fee every time they generate a report on behalf of a merchant, even though they have to provide details about merchant transactions to support their billing activity. This ridiculous practice makes no sense!

REPORTING

Reporting represents the third important facet of cost. Reports should provide invaluable information about how much payment card activity took place in the past reporting period, how much it cost to accept those cards, and most importantly how much you earned by offering customers bankcards as a payment alternative.

There are a myriad of individual report formats available. Unfortunately, the overwhelming majority have been designed by payment card service providers that have little feel or understanding of merchants' unique reporting requirements. There are also a number of report formats that have been specifically designed to obfuscate.

However, every provider maintains the option of providing you, the merchant, with the raw data associated with your payment card activity. As a card-accepting merchant, it's a good idea to work with you accountant and/or bookkeeper to design a customized report that fits your specific business needs. At a minimum, you want to know transaction volumes and dollars transacted with each card brand, along with return and any chargeback information.

You also need the detailed transaction information that supports volume statistics. You need to know the Interchange charge associated with each transaction, presuming you are charged according to the Interchange Plus billing methodology. You also need to know the "plus" portion billed in support of the transaction activity and account maintenance fees. With this information you should be able to calculate the effective rate charged in support of your merchant account.

Chapter 6 | What You Need to Know About PCI and EMV

Security is a paramount concern for everyone involved in payment services, as regular reports of hacking and card frauds make clear. In an effort to contain fraud and hacking, the card companies have imposed two sets of security requirements around credit and debit cards. The Payment Card Industry Data Security Standard (PCI for short) was the first; it was followed by the Europay, MasterCard, Visa chip security initiative (most commonly referred to by the acronym EMV). Here's an overview of what's involved and what you, as a merchant, can do to avoid potentially costly problems from non-compliance.

> *As a card-accepting merchant, YOU MUST complete and file a PCI Self-Assessment Questionnaire, and YOU MUST use POS devices capable of reading EMV chip cards. Not doing so will prove costly.*

First and foremost, you must complete and file a PCI Self-Assessment Questionnaire (SAQ). It doesn't matter how you answer the questions, but not having an SAQ on file can result in hefty non-compliance fees being assessed on a monthly basis.

Additionally, if you have a POS terminal that connects to the Internet in any fashion, the device must be scanned by a third party company authorized to perform PCI compliance scans. Most processors provide scans for all Internet-supported devices automatically, but it is a good idea to verify that your processor actually performs the scans. Positive results purportedly ensure a device has not as yet been hacked. The scan must be repeated on a periodic basis to provide ongoing evidence that devices remain hack free.

As a card-accepting merchant you also must use POS devices that are capable of reading the EMV chips embedded in bank-issued credit and debit cards. Whatever terminal you purchase, be sure it also accepts Apple Pay and other mobile payment options, and that it is capable of encrypting an entire transaction from the first swipe and keystroke through transmission and response. The terminal may seem expensive but, weighed against the potential losses from frauds that might ensue from non-secured transactions, it's significantly less expensive.

PCI

The PCI standards came about in response to a rampant rise in fraud involving stolen card data, many of which could be traced back to repeated hacking of merchant, bank, network and processor data bases. The standards were developed, and continue to be refined by, the PCI Council. Ostensibly, the PCI Council is neutral third party and includes representation from throughout the card industry. In reality, however, Visa and MasterCard run the show. They have the right to amend the standards at will to meet their specific requirements; they also have sole responsibility for assessing and collecting all fines for violations of PCI standards. In fact, these organizations can and have fined innumerable small merchants into non-existence for alleged PCI violations.

*It doesn't really matter how you answer a
PCI Self-Assessment Questionnaire, but you
must answer it!*

Over the years, the body of PCI rules and regulations has swelled to include thousands of pages. They are all completely accessible by any interested party at the PCI Council's website (https://www.pcisecuritystandards.org). They can also be accessed on the Visa and MasterCard websites, along with thousands of pages of additional requirements. No one could possibly successfully wade through all of these documents, but any company that wishes to be involved with accepting and/or processing payments must comply with all of the requirements that pertain to those cards, or face annihilation.

In a twist of irony, small retailers using old dial-up POS terminals that can do very little in terms of providing modern day access to the payment infrastructure actually face the lowest threat level. These old terminals cannot be hacked and are generally exempt from most PCI requirements. The SAQ is required no matter what, however.

The more sophisticated your POS terminal, the greater the risks. Happily, once you install a POS terminal that encrypts transactions you are once again "hack-proof". This, of course, presumes your processor can support some level of encryption. At this time not all processors can, so it's a good idea to include language in your merchant contract requiring some level of encryption. Once you have installed an encryption-capable POS device, you have done just about all you can as a merchant to protect yourself from outside hackers.

Unfortunately, there is little to protect you as a merchant from hacks and other breaches of those organizations that manage the payment system infrastructure. The only way to completely protect yourself is to never, ever, accept any payment card. You may be able to forestall some problems if your service provider offers PCI insurance. This gets tricky, however, in that insurances vary.

With regards to insurance, it is important to determine if the processor provides insurance through a third party, as this may provide a bit more security, assuming the insurer is not a wholly owned subsidiary of the processor. Many providers offer self-insurance, which often means that when it comes time to write a check they may disappear. Others offer "onetime" coverage, which provides coverage for the first card violated and not the entire set of cards hacked. If just one cardholder is violated, the fines assessed could run from $50,000 to $100,000. If large numbers of cards are impacted, multi-million dollar fines should be anticipated. Insurance doesn't typically cover those eventualities. These are important factors to analyze.

It's not just the card brands you have to worry about either, as several states have enacted laws that trigger some amount of fines over and above those assessed by the major card brands for merchants who are victims of card hacks.

An interesting note associated with PCI is that Visa proudly insists that no organization certified as PCI compliant has ever been hacked. Think about that – NEVER! Does that strike anyone as odd? Billions of dollars have been spent by millions of companies to ensure PCI compliance, yet the crooks always seem to target those companies that are not PCI compliant. How is that possible? Is there a list somewhere that only crooks have access to that identify these errant companies? Do they have some sort of mark that sets them apart?

Well, actually they do. Every company that has been breached thus far accepts or processes Visa and MasterCard credit and debit cards. As card-accepting merchants or processors, they are held to Rule 6 of the PCI compliance rules, which requires all participating companies to develop and maintain secure systems and applications. While this rule seems innocuous, it is incredibly nefarious because taken to its logical conclusion it is impossible to ever be PCI compliant. If you, as a merchant, suffer a breach, you have not maintained a secure system or application, therefore you are in violation of Rule 6, and you are not PCI compliant. Now that's a rule!

No wonder Visa is so strident and resolute in its pronouncement. Logically, they are absolutely right. But it doesn't quite ring true. The logic seems out of whack.

Here's another problem with the way PCI compliance plays out. Visa and MasterCard both maintain that they only enforce the rules promulgated by the PCI Council, suggesting they are at arm's length in the process. Yet both are founding and funding members of the PCI Council. Both are also for-profit companies, which means creating shareholder wealth is their prime directive and motivator. Clearly, one way to maximize revenues is to develop a set of standards that cannot be met, thus ensuring a steady flow of income from non-compliance fines.

EMV

EMV cards differ from traditional magnetic-stripe cards in that customer information is encrypted and embedded in a chip that sits on the card. On magnetic striped cards, the customer account information is encoded on the stripe which can easily be read and copied using cloning machines readily available in the marketplace. Because it is encrypted, chip card security is supposed to render cards and readers hack proof by generating transaction data that can only be used once. Unfortunately this has not proven to be the case in Europe, where EMV was pioneered.

EMV is an international security standard that only recently became mandatory in the United States. As of October 2016, following a seven-year lead up, all organizations handling payment cards and card data had to be able to accept and process transactions initiated with cards incorporating EMV chips. Gasoline service stations with pay-at-the-pump technology have until October 2020 to be in compliance. As of this writing about half of all merchants, including a third of small retailers, were said to be EMV compliant.

The incentive for card-issuing banks to migrate to the EMV-compliant chip cards is what the card brands refer to as a "liability shift." As a result of this liability shift, any transactions that are deemed fraudulent as a result of accepting a magnetic stripe card (as opposed to the EMV chip card) become the financial responsibility of you, the merchant, and not the issuing bank, as had been the most common situation previously.

The liability is yours even if the card was issued without an EMV chip, or if your processor has not implemented the infrastructure necessary to accept EMV cards despite you installing EMV capable devices!

With EMV, Visa and MasterCard have shifted liability for card fraud to merchants with impunity.

Evidence readily available from other countries with wide-spread EMV implementations indicates that unless 100% EMV participation is achieved, large scale frauds using magnetic stripe cards still occurs. It is interesting to note that there is no country on the planet that has achieved 100% EMV participation, even though some programs have been running for decades.

It is also worth noting that the primary reason 100% participation has not been achieved is that the entire planet still accepts magnetic stripe cards issued in the U.S. Apparently, tourism, especially involving U.S citizens, represents too attractive a market to ignore on a global basis.

In effect, Visa- and MasterCard-issuing banks have been able to successfully shift their global liability for fraud from themselves to their retailer clients with absolute impunity. In extensive interviews with merchants, I've found few among smaller merchants are even aware of this liability shift. Among larger firms that are aware, most view it as a cost of doing business and have raised prices accordingly.

Despite the many shortcomings associated with EMV, it is imperative as a retailer that you install POS devices capable of accepting EMV chip cards, and that your processor can prove themselves capable of accepting and processing transactions initiated with EMV cards. It may appear expensive but one fraud-based chargeback can wipe out profits earned from accepting any payment card, and do so in a heartbeat. This is all part of survival in the modern era of payment card acceptance.

Chapter 7 | Who's That Knocking at My Door?

If you have been a merchant for a week or two, you have undoubtedly been called upon by more than one salesperson representing a merchant acquirer offering the very lowest card acceptance rates and the very best customer service. It is important to remember the primary goal for any merchant sales representative is to convince you to change providers regardless of whether that truly is the best deal for your business.

Merchant level sales reps are trained to instantly gain your confidence as a merchant and to show you worlds that you never knew existed before. The scary part is that aside from facts like they smile, wear shiny shoes and offer up impressive looking business cards, you really have no idea who you are talking with or who they represent. Even scarier is that at any given moment, neither does the sales rep.

Their job is to get you to change relationships, and although the rep's objective is to convince you to change, which provider gets your business is an open issue at all times to the seasoned sales rep. More often than not, the sales rep is personally driven by a prime directive even more imperative than their goal of eliciting change: making money. The uber-successful sales rep can easily earn seven figures annually and brooks no wasted time or effort.

He (or she) has more than likely sized up your business before even crossing the threshold. They most likely performed a "thumbnail" underwriting sitting outside your business establishment, the results of which determined whether or not the rep's primary acquirer will approve your application. If so, all is well. If not, the rep will typically have an ongoing relationship with an alternative acquirer that will approve your business, albeit at a less attractive rate.

Sales reps are trained to gain your confidence. Their primary goal is to get you to switch bankcard services providers, even if it's not a good deal for your particular business.

One of the vagaries of the business is that most merchant sales reps are entities unto themselves, even though they may be contractually pledged to represent a specific acquirer. It is worth noting that uber-sales reps, known in the industry as "closers," represent the top 5% of all sales reps. Closers and high-performers combined represent about 20% of any given sales force and, together, these reps generate 80% of all merchant sales. Their sole motivation is commissions: the more merchants they can sign the better their cash flow. High performers can be trained, but closers represent a personality type that is a natural phenomenon; they are born with the talent.

There are a number of different types of sales reps who are likely to call on you as a merchant, and they can be there on behalf of any of several different types of businesses. Here's a short list followed by brief descriptions.

- ISO sales rep
- Independent contractor representing an ISO
- Independent contractor representing a sub ISO to the primary ISO
- ISO telemarketer
- Value-Added Reseller (VAR) sales rep
- Front-End Processor (FEP) sales rep
- Hardware sales rep
- Gateway sales rep
- Acquirer/merchant bank direct sales rep

ISO SALES REP

An ISO sales rep works directly for an ISO. They likely earn some sort of base salary in combination with a commission structure. They are often motivated to sell on behalf of the ISO by the security of a stable paycheck combined with the opportunity for substantially higher income based on performance. Minimum performance standards usually ensure at least minimal output. Many reps are attracted to this position having faced the reality they are neither closers nor top performers. They are generally very competent but not driven.

INDEPENDENT CONTRACTOR REPRESENTING AN ISO

An Independent Contractor (IC) is self-employed, making their services available to ISOs on a pure commission basis. The more they sell, the more money they make. Many ISOs prefer to use ICs as they cost nothing to support, short of business cards. Most closers and high performers are ICs, but the obverse is not necessarily the case. ICs often represent more than one provider at a time, although rarely disclosing their status while pledging undying loyalty to each and every provider they represent.

Closers thrive in a pure commission environment. Run of the mill ICs are often known as "trunk slammers," a derogatory term referring their habit of carrying their terminals and equipment in the trunk of their cars, slamming it shut when they are disgruntled and don't make sales.

ISO TELEMARKETER

ISO telemarketers generally work within the huge telemarketing operations of an acquiring organization. They "dial for dollars" all day long using extensive lists of business phone numbers. They follow carefully engineered scripts designed to pry important information from individual merchants like you that they can use to generate follow-up visits from sales reps. This process obviates the need for cold calls and dramatically increases the ratio of visits to closes by sales reps. The telemarketer has evolved into an effective lead-generating mechanism within the merchant acquiring business, and a good telephone "closer" is worth their weight in gold.

VALUE-ADDED RESELLER SALES REP

A Value-added Reseller (VAR) sales rep can be a valuable ally, or not, depending upon circumstance. In merchant card acquiring a VAR is a software or hardware provider that installs integrated POS systems or software application packages that run on systems already in place. The sales rep can be an invaluable source of industry-specific information, presuming the VAR has extensive knowledge of your specific market niche. Problems can arise, however, if a VAR tries to append a payment application onto their software package to make it more attractive without the requisite payment systems expertise. It may be worthwhile to call your accountant or bookkeeper for input when considering any new payment application a VAR sales rep may offer.

FRONT-END PROCESSOR SALES REP

As a small merchant, it is unlikely you will be visited by a Front-end Processor (FEP) sales rep, but it's not out of the question. FEPs often have internal sales forces, and most focus on national accounts that oversee very large clients with thousands of locations. The development of industry specific POS applications may prompt more sales activities into smaller merchant markets by FEPs.

HARDWARE SALES REP

Several POS terminal manufacturers have developed proprietary FEP platforms and have tasked their sales forces (as well as select ISOs) to sell access to those platforms. Their logic is that the sales rep is going into your store anyway, so they may as well have something else to offer. Other hardware manufacturers have agreements under which select FEPs gain access to their platforms on a more or less exclusive basis for a share of the revenue generated. This represents a win-win for both parties.

GATEWAY SALES REP

There are a number of gateway owners that are also ISOs, and some ISOs have their own gateways. A gateway is incredibly interested in signing you up as a merchant because that puts them in control of where your transactions get sent. FEPs and acquirers are always on the lookout for groups of merchants that are represented by a single party. That party, in this case the gateway, can strike a more lucrative deal if they bring a lot of merchants to the table. Many of their contracts contain language that allows gateway owners to deal on your behalf, so be sure to carefully review any contracts with gateways before signing on.

ACQUIRER/MERCHANT BANK DIRECT SALES REP

An acquirer/merchant bank direct sales rep is a regular employee of an acquirer or merchant bank. Their primary focus is selling access to the bank or acquirer network. Most direct sale reps are assigned to the "national" accounts department. Taking a national client from a competitor is a big deal in payment services, but as a small merchant the only interaction you'll likely have with a national accounts rep is as a customer in your store. Many acquirers and banks outsource small account sales efforts to ISOs or have acquired ISOs as subsidiaries.

An exception to this is where the acquirer has developed expertise and accompanying technology to support specific merchant types. Examples would include retailers that specialize in auto parts, ski resorts or bowling alleys. An acquirer will often field a sales force that has industry-specific knowledge and can speak to unique needs of a specific group of merchant customers.

These sales reps are typically more professional in their approach and generally are not closers.

Asking the right questions is key to your survival as a merchant when dealing with card services sales reps.

Irrespective of who is selling to you, the merchant, on any given day, it is important as part of your survival training to make sure you ask the right questions of any sales rep that seeks your card business. This will help ensure the continued success of your business.

Chapter 8 | And Along Came the Disruptors

As industries mature, solutions tend to develop across providers that fit within existing technologies and tend to get applied across a wide spectrum of potential customers to maximize profitability. The payments industry is no exception. Big players come to rely on big solutions. Custom solutions that fit smaller needs have been left to the VAR community, but even their solutions tend to fit the existing technological infrastructure. Even innovation finds itself restrained by the status quo.

As with other industries, however, innovators with imagination and huge personal or corporate resources come along and shake things up. Payments innovators have developed not only entirely new technological approaches to processing transactions, but have attacked the long held pricing mechanism by offering better, faster and/or cheaper alternatives.

Aggregation models are upending traditional merchant-acquirer relationships

The impact of these companies has been so dramatic they have been tagged as disruptors. Apple, PayPal and Square are the most widely recognized disruptors. They have upended the traditional business model whereby each card-accepting merchant had to individually contract with a merchant-acquiring bank. This in turn led to a new business model where card acceptance is only one feature in sophisticated integrated solutions.

Integrated software providers use advanced technologies to enhance onboarding, fraud detection and other aspects of card acceptance, and often focus on specific vertical markets, such as digital commerce, personal care, fitness and personal transportation businesses. By aggregating client transactions for processing through a master merchant card-acquiring account, these companies are able to support more simplified and lower pricing.

Historically, card brand rules prohibited the aggregation of card transactions from multiple merchants for processing through a single account, but those rules began to change in 2011. Today, all of the major card brands allow for "master merchants" that aggregate and process card transactions for "sub-merchants." Card brand rules limit sub-merchant activity to processing $1 million per card brand per year under these aggregation models.

There are three disruptors included in this book, although there are yet other, smaller disruptors already in the marketplace and many more on the way. Two of those included have disrupted pricing and delivery, and one provides an evolving payment medium.

It must be pointed out that this book does not endorse any of the disruptors discussed in this chapter, and each should be thoroughly analyzed and vetted along with any other providers you as a merchant may consider for meeting your payment processing needs.

SQUARE

Square's greatest appeal is its simplified approach to pricing, ease of sign-up and technology. There is a time honored business axiom that posits it is impossible to lose money on every sale and make it up in volume. Square appears to be the exception that proves that rule. With a market capitalization approaching $16 billion and 8 years in the marketplace, Square has yet to turn a profit on transaction processing activities, according to the company's financial reports.

This lack of profitability arises from the fact that Square charges a flat 2.75% per swiped, dipped or tapped transaction and 3.5% plus 15 cents for keyed-in transactions. Those rates apply across the spectrum of popular card brands, and there are no monthly or hidden fees.

Square makes the merchant application process incredibly easy. And it's online. Plus, it typically provides card-reading dongles for free; Square chip card readers are priced at $29. As master merchant, Square is responsible for PCI compliance, which frees individual merchants from the need to complete a Self-Assessment Questionnaires and other PCI-related hassles. Square merchants also receive free chargeback protection, as well as payment dispute and other assistance immediately online, or via phone, email or Twitter. Plus, merchant deposits are available in one to two business days, or on a same-day for a 1% fee (subject to restrictions).

While profitability remains elusive, Square managed a successful IPO in 2015. It has also launched a number of ancillary lines of business including:

- same-day funding (referenced above and known as Instant Deposit);
- a virtual platform to support ecommerce for physical merchants (Square Market)
- Square Cash/Cash Pro, both fee-based person-to-person payment platforms.

Square also offers Square Register, the big brother to its iPhone/iPad-based services along with a new generation of EMV card-reading devices, and a reader that supports Apple Pay.

Square Capital, launched in 2014, had extended well over $1 billion in capital to over 100,000 small merchants as of 2017. Additional initiatives include an expanding selection of industry-specific business solutions including food and beverage, health and beauty, service and repair, general retail and more than a dozen others.

Available business management tools include, but are not limited to a dashboard to track activity, in-depth analytics, personnel management, location management, payroll, inventory control, customer directory and engagement. Additional products and services include e-commerce, gift cards, debit cards and Caviar, a food ordering and delivery service. All of these cross-selling opportunities add significant revenues to Square's balance sheet, and the company has promised innovations going forward.

Square has many pros; terms of service may not be one of those.

Square often touts the fact that no contracts are required to use its card-acceptance service. Although this is true, every user is subject to an incredibly lengthy, convoluted and confusing Terms of Service.

Here is one ominous paragraph found at the beginning of Square's Terms of Service:

By using any of the Services you agree to these General Terms and any policies referenced within ("Policies"), including terms that limit our liability (see Section 18) and require individual arbitration for any potential legal dispute (see

Section 21). You also agree to any additional terms specific to Services you use ("Additional Terms"), such as those listed below, which become part of your agreement with us. You should read all of our terms carefully.

The Term of Service also append over a dozen additional specialized Terms of Agreements, each of which is also incredibly lengthy, convoluted and confusing, that the user must adhere to without benefit of a contractual agreement. Special care should be taken when reviewing these. You may want to consider consulting an attorney before agreeing to any of these Terms of Service, especially the one designated The Commercial Entity agreement.

As is pointed out elsewhere in this book, if everything goes well and nothing breaks, none of these Terms of Service agreements are of concern. It is when things break or go south do they take on import. Caveat emptor!

PAYPAL

With a market capitalization today of around $91 billion, PayPal is one of the largest Internet companies supporting ecommerce services for on-line retailers and a number of on-line auction sites. Its origins trace back to a group of Silicon Valley luminaries: Elon Musk, Peter Thiel, Max Levchin, Ken Howery, Luke Nosek, and Yu Pan. The company at one point was owned by eBay and provided all payment services for that auction site. Following its spin-off from eBay in 2015, PayPal ventured into providing services for brick-and-mortar retailers, and supporting all types of merchants, from the largest to small mom-and-pop shops. The company claims more than 200 million people use PayPal to pay for purchases at over 17 million businesses.

PayPal supports acceptance of all major card brands as well as payments from PayPal accounts. The company imposes no sign up or cancellation fees, and offers attractive per-transaction pricing. It also offers credit services and alternative payment solutions tailored to specific merchant segments.

Unlike Square, PayPal requires contracts, but per-transaction pricing is attractive

PayPal charges online merchants a flat fee of 2.9% of the transaction amount plus 30-cents for payments from domestic customers; transactions originating from outside the U.S. are assessed a 4.4% flat fee plus a currency conversion fee. Fees for brick and mortar generated payments are assessed at a rate of 2.7% of the transaction amount when the card is swiped; and 3.5% of the ticket plus 15-cents for manually-entered transactions. Micro-merchants with transactions under $10 pay 5% of the transaction amount. Charitable organizations pay 2.2% of the transaction amount.

PayPal-Pro is a virtual terminal offering with its own pricing structure, which includes a monthly fee. There's also a PayPal version of smartphone-based POS systems.

Unlike Square, PayPal does require a contract, the main body of which is 47 pages long. PayPal also has four additional agreements which all customers must sign and 26 other agreements that may pertain to your company. It may be worthwhile to secure the services of a competent attorney to help determine which of these pertain to your business in order to protect against any potentially onerous or life threatening clauses these may contain.

APPLE PAY

Apple Pay is perhaps the best known of many emerging smartphone-based payment alternatives. Like all other emerging smartphone-based payment offerings, it has been given minimal marketing support from its parent company. With a market capitalization of about $875 billion, Apple is the largest company in the payments industry. The Apple Pay initiative represents a miniscule investment of that capital base, while representing a huge potential for large and small merchants alike.

Apple's customer base is estimated at just over 1.1 billion worldwide, and every one of those customers has an iTunes account. iPhone users total 650 million worldwide, and Apple is offering merchants access to many of these consumers through the Apple Pay program. Obviously it is not as simple a prospect as it sounds.

---

*Accepting Apple Pay is not as simple a
prospect as it might seem for merchants*

In order to fulfill the opportunity, Apple must convince its iPhone customers to activate the Apple Pay feature, which is available only on iPhone 6 or newer devices. Apple must simultaneously convince you, the merchant, to convince customers to use Apple Pay on your POS devices. And that's not all: your merchant processor must be capable of supporting Apple Pay and your POS device must be Near Field Communications (NFC) compliant and thus capable of accepting contactless payments. This in turn may require changing your merchant processor, upgrading POS devices or at a minimum upgrading device software.

Apple Pay is highlighted here because it is the most mature of the mobile payment offerings in the market today. The transaction is absolutely secure, unlike virtually every other alternative available to merchants. The customer's account number is nowhere to be found and the transaction is only authorized with the customer's face ID, fingerprint or passcode. Apple Pay supports all payment card brands.

There are no additional fees for accepting Apple Pay transactions. To start accepting Apple Pay, contact your

ISO or merchant services provider and ask them to activate the service. It is that simple. They handle the rest. You will need signage to let your customers know that you accept the service.

Should your merchant provider not be cooperative, you can reach Apple Pay customer service from the Apple Pay website (https://www.apple.com/apple-pay/).

Chapter 9 | Things to Inquire About and Consider – A Review

The following list of questions was originally presented as part of the Smart Retailer's Checklist as those that you should ask before considering accepting payment cards or while searching for a new payment processing relationship. They are of such critical importance to your survival as a merchant, you should take yet another look. They are therefore offered again for your review. Please remember that as a smart retailer, it is in your best interests to ask questions, challenge the answers and ask again. This is about your livelihood.

1. **What pricing model does the provider offer?** It should be Interchange Plus. If it isn't, insist the provider change to Interchange Plus as soon as it is practical to do so. If you are being charged according to any other pricing model, you are likely being cheated. Even Interchange Plus isn't bulletproof, but it is the most transparent and fair model available today. Have an attorney ensure contractually the processor uses the actual

published interchange rates for their calculations. Some are known to make up rates.

2. **Does the provider supply reports that break down transaction numbers and amounts by each applicable interchange rate?** This is the only way to truly ascertain how much is being charged. It may be wise to ask for the raw data and have your accountant or bookkeeper write a spreadsheet program that displays it all in an easy to read format. Also, make sure the "plus" portion applied to each Interchange rate appears reasonable, although reasonable can be a flexible term.

3. **What other fees are billed on a monthly basis, and are there any fees not billed monthly? If so, what are they, how often are they billed and how are they presented on reports?** Be sure to obtain a thorough list of all extraneous charges levied by the various parties involved providing your business with merchant services and how they are reported. Take time to understand what each term means as they can change based on context. If necessary, keep asking questions. If nothing else, you can revel in the fact that you are slowly driving your provider crazy. But seriously, it's important to get a handle on all-in costs, including

potentially hidden items that can add up over time.

4. **Does the processor support some effective type of data encryption? If not, when will it be available and fully implemented?** Having a way to prevent data from being read while in transit could save you from losing everything you own because of data breaches. As a merchant, you need a processor that supports some type of solid encryption methodology and your contract should reflect the processor's obligation to do that. Some providers have been known to lie about security capabilities which merchants realize only after being hacked.

5. **Are all installed POS devices PCI compliant? Do they support EMV card acceptance, end-to-end encryption, Apple Pay and emerging mobile payment applications?** If the answer to any of these questions is no, immediately upgrade to a POS device that meets these requirements, even if it appears incredibly expensive. A POS device meeting these requirements, when coupled with a processor that actually supports end-to-end encryption, could end up saving your business from financial annihilation from fines and other breach-related costs.

6. **What is the timeframe between when POS terminal(s) get settled and when the funds actually post to your business account?** These monies are referred to as "holdbacks," and the timeframe these funds are held can vary dramatically from a couple of days to a month. Processors claim holdbacks provide a level of security against potential chargebacks and possible fraud. Some processors offer same day funding but typically charge significant premiums for the service. It wouldn't hurt to find out the cost and calculate the benefits and costs of gaining access to your funds faster.

7. **How frequently does the processor perform PCI scans, and what does it cost?** Presuming your installed POS device(s) is not a dial-up terminal, PCI scans for vulnerabilities will be performed automatically by the processor and you will be charged accordingly. Find out how often they are performed, by who, and how much you are charged per scan.

8. **Is it absolutely required to complete and submit a PCI Self-Assessment Questionnaire (SAQ)?** As a card-accepting merchant you must complete the PCI SAQ even if your answers may not make sense. The SAQ offers you, the merchant, absolutely no protection in and of itself, but

completing it could save you a ton of money in monthly penalties.

9. **How much are you charged if you do not submit an SAQ?** Processors typically charge a fine of $50 per month until the SAQ is submitted. ISOs have been known to tack on additional fees as well. You may want to determine the fines have been removed upon submission as some conveniently forget to do so when required.

10. **If PCI insurance is provided, who provides it, how much does it cost, and what exactly does it cover?** Many processors and ISOs offer PCI insurance but a number of these insurance plans come with conditions that render them almost useless. For example are those plans that cover a single incident only. Most data breaches include thousands of payment cards and each card is considered a single incident. Some providers offer self-insured PCI insurance plans providing an out by merely declaring bankruptcy if the incident become too large to cover.

11. **What are the procedures and costs associated with cancelling an existing contract? In particular, what are the charges for early termination?** The specific procedures and costs are typically provided in the Terms & Conditions

document referenced in the Merchant Processing Agreement. Be sure to request a copy of the T&C before signing any agreement. Some processors apply incredibly onerous penalties for merchants that terminate contracts early. The upward range could reach tens of thousands of dollars. Currently only one state, Arkansas, actually caps the termination fee ($50) but most providers ignore the statute as it carries no penalties for violation. Check the statutes for states where you operate as this movement may gain traction.

12. **What are the financial consequences of falling short of or grossly exceeding expected monthly transaction volumes?** Many contracts require minimum monthly payments even in months when no card transactions get processed. At the other end of the spectrum, a merchant that dramatically exceeds expectations will trigger alarms with processors, as huge volume spikes typically are associated with large scale frauds. There have been cases uncovered in the past in which fraudsters were able to run millions of dollars in transactions through individual small merchants in a matter of seconds. It is important to note that as the merchant, you are most likely responsible for these transactions and any associated fees and penalties, which could amount to millions of dollars. Many states have passed

laws that also include provisions that could lead to incarceration in such cases.

13. **How and where are funds received from your daily card transactions deposited?** If they are being deposited into your primary business checking account, you may want to open a new account at a different bank to receive those funds. You will also want to move the funds from that secondary account as soon as they are deposited, as merchant banks and Independent Sales Organizations (ISOs) cannot seize funds they cannot access.

14. **How are routine customer service issues handled?** This industry is fairly benign and for the most part everything works as it should. It is important, however, to know who to call after you're up and running and things do not go as planned. You need to know how to escalate things should it become necessary. All processors provide call center support, some using dedicated in-house staff while others outsource the capability. This is important to know, as in-house resources tend to be a bit more responsive to client needs.

As noted throughout this book, the devil is in the details. I am convinced that there are many more details concerning this simple looking, yet incredibly complicated business that have escaped my attention and therefore inclusion in this book. This is all about YOUR money and card processing is not necessarily your particular forte. Even the very smartest among us needs some assistance at times. My sincere hope is that I have provided at least some insight. Best of luck!

About the Author

Paul Martaus is the president and CEO of Martaus & Associates, a company he founded in 1990, which specializes in electronic payment systems research consulting and professional education in the payment card transaction acquiring space.

Prior to forming Martaus & Associates, Mr. Martaus was the director of research for Payment Systems, Inc. (PSI), a financial services research and consulting company. At PSI, he performed consumer and industry research covering all aspects of delivering financial services to consumers, financial institutions, merchants and the government.

Mr. Martaus has over 35 years of direct banking operations and EFT experience and was an SVP of a bank when he was 26 years old. In addition, he was the COO of a privately owned ATM network, the Neighborhood Banking Centers, and held management, marketing and technical positions at two major electronic banking software companies.

Mr. Martaus resides in Mountain Home, Arkansas.